PAIRED PASSAGES

Grade 5

Credits
Content Editor: Kristina L. Biddle
Copy Editor: Carrie D'Ascoli

Visit *carsondellosa.com* for correlations to Common Core, state, national, and Canadian provincial standards.

Carson-Dellosa Publishing, LLC
PO Box 35665
Greensboro, NC 27425 USA
carsondellosa.com

ISBN 978-1-4838-3069-8
01-067161151

Table of Contents

Introduction

As students sharpen their reading comprehension skills, they become better readers. Improving these skills has never been more important as teachers struggle to meet the rigorous college- and career-ready expectations of today's educational standards.

This book offers pairings of high-interest fiction and nonfiction passages that will appeal to even the most reluctant readers. The passages have grade-level readability. Follow-up pages promote specific questioning based on evidence from the passages.

Throughout the book, students are encouraged to practice close reading, focusing on details to make inferences from each passage separately and then as a set. The text-dependent questions and activities that follow the passages encourage students to synthesize the information they have read, leading to deeper comprehension.

How to Use This Book

Three types of pairings divide this book: fiction with nonfiction, nonfiction with nonfiction, and fiction with fiction. The book is broken down further into 22 sets of paired passages that are combined with follow-up questions and activities. Each reading passage is labeled *Fiction* or *Nonfiction*.

The passages in this book may be used in any order but should be completed as four-page sets so that students read the passages in the correct pairs. The pairs of passages have been carefully chosen and each pair has topics or elements in common.

Two pages of questions and activities follow each pair of passages to support student comprehension. The questions and activities are based on evidence that students can find in the texts. No further research is required. Students will answer a set of questions that enable comprehension of each of the two passages. The questions range in format and include true/false, multiple choice, and short answer. The final questions or activities ask students to compare and contrast details or elements from the two passages.

Assessment Rubric

Use this rubric as a guide for assessing students' work. It can also be offered to students to help them check their work or as a tool to show your scoring.

4	
	_____ Independently reads and comprehends grade-level texts
	_____ Easily compares and contrasts authors' purposes
	_____ Uses higher order thinking skills to link common themes or ideas
	_____ References both passages when comparing and contrasting
	_____ Skillfully summarizes reading based on textual evidence

3	
	_____ Needs little support for comprehension of grade-level texts
	_____ Notes some comparisons of authors' purposes
	_____ Infers broad common themes or ideas
	_____ Connects the key ideas and general theme of both passages
	_____ Uses textual evidence to summarize reading with some support

2	
	_____ Needs some support for comprehension of grade-level texts
	_____ Understands overt similarities in authors' purposes
	_____ Links stated or obvious common themes or ideas
	_____ Compares and contrasts both passages with support
	_____ Summarizes reading based on textual evidence with difficulty

1	
	_____ Reads and comprehends grade-level text with assistance
	_____ Cannot compare or contrast authors' purposes
	_____ Has difficulty linking common themes or ideas
	_____ Cannot connect the information from both passages
	_____ Is unable to use textual evidence to summarize reading

The Road Not Taken
by Robert Frost

Two roads **diverged** in a yellow wood,
And sorry I could not travel both
And be one traveler, long I stood
And looked down one as far as I could
To where it bent in the undergrowth;

Then took the other, as just as fair,
And having perhaps the better claim,
Because it was grassy and wanted wear;
Though as for that the passing there
Had worn them really about the same,

And both that morning equally lay
In leaves no step had trodden black.
Oh, I kept the first for another day!
Yet knowing how way leads on to way,
I doubted if I should ever come back.

I shall be telling this with a sigh
Somewhere ages and ages hence:
Two roads diverged in a wood, and I—
I took the one less traveled by,
And that has made all the difference.

This or That?

People make a number of decisions every day. Many of these decisions are easy, but others are very difficult. Even children make decisions every day: which clothing to wear to school, what to eat for lunch, who to play with during recess, which answers to select on a test, and whether to join in or help when someone is being bullied.

Some decisions you make involve problems, and your choices may lead to consequences. If you ever have a difficult time deciding what to do, try using any of these strategies:

1. Think about it. Do you need to find out more? If so, do some research.

2. Brainstorm as many solutions as you can.

3. Think about the consequences of each solution. Are they good or bad? Who will be involved in the results, and how will everyone feel?

4. Think with both your mind and your heart; listen to your body. Is your heart beating fast? Are your palms sweating? These signs might mean that you are worried or scared about your choice.

5. Is a right or wrong decision obvious? Often, you know what you should do but are afraid of what someone else may think. Discuss it with a family member or a trusted adult and find out what they recommend.

6. Make a decision and stick to it. Accept any consequences that may happen as a result of your decision.

Most decisions we make are not extremely important. Perhaps this list will help you make the ones that are.

Name _____

Answer the questions.

1. In what genre is "The Road Not Taken"? How do you know?

   _____

   _____

2. How is "This or That" organized? How do you know?

   _____

   _____

3. How do you think the narrator in "The Road Not Taken" feels about the decision that was made? Use evidence to support your answer.

   _____

   _____

   _____

4. Which season is it in "The Road Not Taken"? Use at least two pieces of evidence from the passage to support your answer.

   _____

   _____

   _____

5. What is the main idea of "This or That"? Which details support the main idea?

   _____

   _____

   _____

6. What does the word **diverged** mean as it is used in "The Road Not Taken"?

   A. appeared   **B.** disappeared   **C.** separated   **D.** joined

7. Think about what you learned about making decisions from both passages. Use that information to complete the organizer.

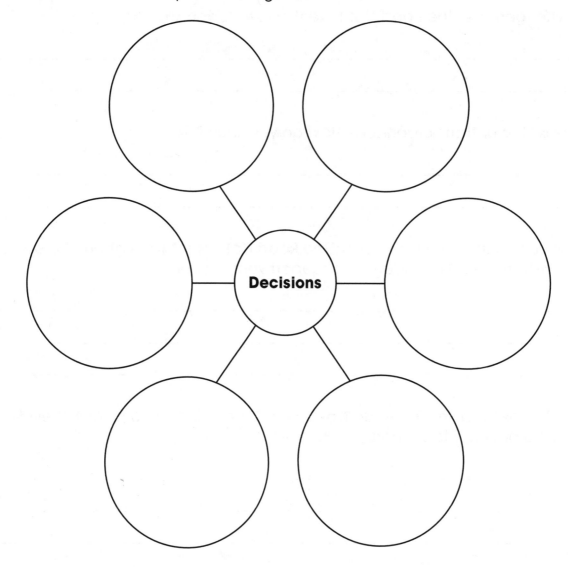

Decisions

8. Pretend that you are the narrator in "The Road Not Taken," and you are using the list from "This or That" to make your decision. Write a journal entry to record your thoughts and how you came to your decision.

_____

_____

_____

_____

_____

_____

The Wind and the Moon
by George Macdonald

1 Said the Wind to the Moon, "I will blow
   you out,

2 You stare in the air like a ghost in a chair,

3 Always looking what I am about—

4 I hate to be watched; I'll blow you out."

5 The Wind blew hard, and out went
   the Moon.

6 So, deep on a heap of clouds to sleep,

7 Down lay the Wind, and slumbered soon,

8 Muttering low, "I've done for that Moon."

9 He turned in his bed; she was there again!

10 On high in the sky, with her one ghost eye,

11 The Moon shone white and alive and plain.

12 Said the Wind, "I will blow you out again."

13 The Wind blew hard, and the Moon
   grew dim.

14 "With my sledge, and my wedge, I have
   knocked off her edge!

15 If only I blow right fierce and grim,

16 The creature will soon be dimmer
   than dim."

17 He blew and he blew, and she thinned to
   a thread.

18 "One puff more's enough to blow her
   to snuff!

19 One good puff more where the last
   was bred,

20 And glimmer, glimmer, glum will go the
   thread."

21 He blew a great blast, and the thread
   was gone.

22 In the air nowhere was a moonbeam bare;

23 Far off and harmless the shy stars shone—

24 Sure and certain the Moon was gone!

25 The Wind he took to his revels once more;

26 On down, in town, like a merry-mad clown,

27 He leaped and hallooed with whistle and
   roar—

28 "What's that?" The glimmering thread
   once more!

29 He flew in a rage—he danced and blew;

30 But in vain was the pain of his bursting brain;

31 For still the broader the Moon—scrap grew,

32 The broader he swelled his big cheeks
   and blew.

33 Slowly she grew—till she filled the night,

34 And shone on her throne in the sky alone,

35 A matchless, wonderful silvery light,

36 Radiant and lovely, the queen of the night.

37 Said the Wind: "What a marvel of power
   am I!

38 With my breath, good faith! I blew her to
   death—

39 First blew her away right out of the sky—

40 Then blew her in; what strength have I!"

41 But the Moon she knew nothing about
   the affair;

42 For high in the sky, with her one white eye,

43 Motionless, miles above the air,

44 She had never heard the great Wind blare.

The Phases of the Moon

Earth's moon goes through multiple phases each month. During this time, the moon's position in relation to the sun and Earth determines how much of it we can see at night.

New Moon

During this stage, the moon is between Earth and the sun. Because the sun is on the other side of the moon, we cannot see it at all. It has totally disappeared because of the sun's brightness.

Third Quarter Moon

This happens as the moon moves closer to the sun. The moon is "waning," or getting smaller each night. The name is derived from the fact that it is three-quarters of the way through the lunar month. From Earth, it appears to be a half-moon, with the left side illuminated by the sun.

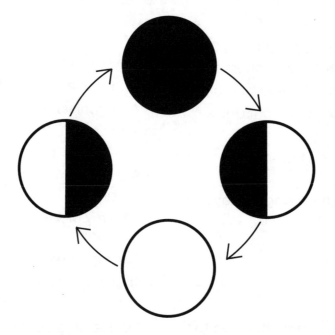

First Quarter Moon

This happens as the moon moves away from the sun. The moon is "waxing," or getting larger each night. The name is derived from the fact that it is one-quarter of the way through its lunar month. From Earth, it appears to be a half-moon, with the right side **illuminated** by the sun.

Full Moon

As it continues to wax, we call it a gibbous moon. It grows larger and larger each night, until we can see the full face of the moon. This is called a full moon.

Name _____

Answer the questions.

1. What is the theme of "The Wind and the Moon"?

   _____

   _____

2. How does the author support the theme in "The Wind and the Moon"?

   _____

   _____

3. What is the structure of "The Phases of the Moon"?

   A. chronology

   B. comparison

   C. problem/solution

   D. cause/effect

4. Which features did the author of "The Phases of the Moon" include to help you better understand the passage?

   _____

   _____

5. What does the word **illuminated** mean as used in "The Phases of the Moon"? What context clues helped you figure it out?

   _____

   _____

6. Think about the Wind. Choose three of the following character traits to describe the Wind and provide text evidence to support your thinking.

   angry   helpful   determined   happy   prideful

   _____

   _____

   _____

7. Think about the phases of the moon based on information from "Phases of the Moon." For each phase, write the numbers of the stanzas from "The Wind and the Moon" that apply to each phase.

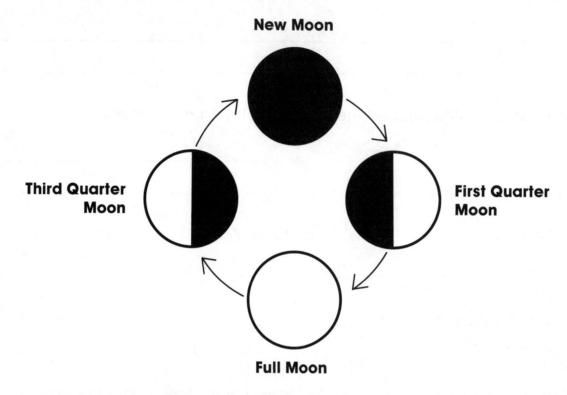

New Moon

Third Quarter Moon

First Quarter Moon

Full Moon

8. Write a letter to the Wind to explain why his thinking is wrong. Use evidence from both passages in your letter.

_____

_____

_____

_____

_____

_____

_____

_____

_____

_____

Bullies

Have you ever been teased by a friend or family member? Most of us have, and it is funny when it is done in a playful, friendly way. We even laugh and tease back! However, when someone teases in an unkind or rude way and refuses to stop, teasing becomes bullying.

Bullies can **torment** in several ways: demanding money, kicking, hitting, name-calling, or spreading rumors. With the popularity of social media, brand-new ways to bully are prevalent. Nearly every child has either witnessed bullying or been bullied.

If you or someone you know is being bullied, keep several things in mind. First, don't fight back or laugh at the bully. This can very quickly make the situation worse. Instead, try any or all of the following tips:

Tell someone! Friends, family members, teachers, a bus driver, or another adult can step in to help. Let them.

Talk it through with someone you trust. This could be a sibling, the guidance counselor at school, or your teacher. They may have some good advice. Even if they do not, it always helps to talk to someone.

Avoid the bully when possible. If you see the bully and you are alone, go the other way. Take someone with you when you know you will see that person. If someone you know is being bullied, offer to stay close.

Do not respond in anger. It is human nature to get upset, but that is really what the bully is hoping for. Find something that helps, such as counting to 10, writing in a journal, or taking deep breaths, and then practice it.

Ignore the bully. If that is impossible, tell him or her to stop in a firm voice and then walk away.

Trouble at School

From: Lindsey
To: Aunt Sally
Sent: Monday, October 12, 3:55 pm
Subject: Miss you!

Dear Aunt Sally,

I wish you didn't have to move so far away! I miss you every day. It's just not the same when I get home and you're not here anymore. Lauren is great and everything, but she's just not you. I hope you're having fun in college and making a lot of new friends.

Remember last year when I talked to you about Emma and the other girls? Well, they're back again this year and being even meaner than before. I tripped on the curb last week and fell into a mud puddle. Emma took a picture, texted it to everyone, and then posted it on the Internet.

Now, everyone at school is laughing at me, and Emma keeps calling me names. I finally had enough and pushed her down. Then, when she fell, my friend took a picture of her. I laughed and said, "How does that feel?" Of course, the teacher came over, and I got in trouble. She called my parents when I refused to tell her why I did it, though. Mom and Dad kept pressuring me to talk to them too. They noticed I'd been crying at night in my room. They wouldn't understand. I just want all of this to go away.

When are you coming home for break? I can't wait! There are a lot of new movies that I want to see and maybe we can go shopping at the mall.

Love you,

Lindsey

Name _____

Answer the questions.

1. What does the word **torment** mean as used in "Bullies"?

   A. tease

   B. act

   C. mistreat

   D. help

2. What is the difference between teasing and bullying?

   _____

   _____

   _____

3. How does the author of "Bullies" support the idea that you should not fight back or laugh at a bully?

   A. by encouraging you to talk to someone

   B. by stating that it will make the situation worse

   C. by telling you to ignore the bully

   D. by suggesting that you tell the bully, "NO"

4. Based on the "Trouble at School" email, why do you think Lindsey responded to the bully the way she did?

   _____

   _____

   _____

5. Do you think Lindsey made the situation better or worse? Explain your thinking.

   _____

   _____

   _____

   _____

Name _____

6. Think about "Trouble at School" and the actions that Emma and Lindsey took. What were the consequences of those actions? How could Emma and Lindsey have handled things differently? Use "Bullies" as a guide to help you complete the chart.

Action	Consequence	An Action That Would Have Been Better

7. Using the chart, as well as the suggestions in "Bullies," write an email back to Lindsey to give her advice on what she should do now.

_____

_____

_____

_____

_____

_____

_____

_____

_____

The Liberty Bell

In 1751, the colonial government ordered a bell for its new State House in Philadelphia. The bell arrived in 1752. The metal used to make the bell caused it to be too brittle. It cracked during the first strike. The bell had to be recast twice. The final bell weighed over 2,000 pounds (907 kg). It was 12 feet (3.67 m) in circumference and 3 feet (0.9 m) tall.

On July 8, 1776, the new bell was rung for the first time. It was in celebration of America's Declaration of Independence. When Britain invaded Philadelphia, the bell was hidden in a church to keep it safe. After the war, it was returned to the State House. It was not until the 1830s that it was actually called the "Liberty Bell."

So, how did the bell get its famous crack? No one knows for certain. There are a few legends. Some say it cracked in 1824 when Revolutionary War hero Marquis de Lafayette visited the city. Others say it happened in 1824 while being used to toll a warning for a fire. Others claim it cracked during Chief Justice John Marshall's funeral in 1835.

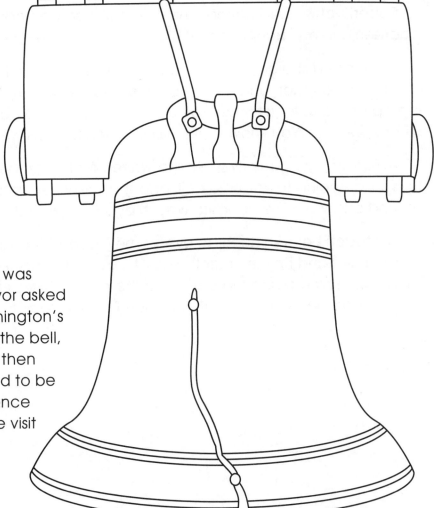

All we know for sure is that it was cracked by 1846 when the mayor asked that it be rung on George Washington's birthday. People tried to repair the bell, and it tolled at first. However, it then cracked beyond repair and had to be retired. It now sits in Independence Center where millions of people visit it each year.

Oops!

Do you ever wonder what children did for fun 100 or even 200 years ago, long before video games or TV were invented? Here's what happened to two children playing the old and forever popular game of hide-and-seek.

Abigail and Robert were running through the kitchen when Mama asked them to finish their game outside. She was afraid something would break, and they knew that their father, the local minister, would be upset with them. His feeling was that children should be seen and not heard. The children ran outside.

"Your turn to seek!" Abigail called to Robert, as she took off running toward the church.

Robert sighed and covered his eyes as he started counting. "One, two, three . . . nineteen, twenty! Here I come!"

He headed straight into the church. He knew Abigail, and he knew her ritual. She was much younger, and she always went to the same place. He should probably at least pretend to look for her, so he wandered around calling out as he went. "Abigail, where are you? You know I'll find you, so you may as well give up and come out now!"

Abigail giggled quietly while she waited for Robert behind the large church bell. He was creeping toward the bell, and she knew her time was up. Suddenly, he turned around and went the opposite way. Maybe she would be lucky and win this time!

"I'll teach her to hide there every time," Robert thought. He reached out to grab the large mallet and hit the church bell. At exactly the same time, two things happened: Abigail screamed, and the bottom of the bell cracked just a little. Robert turned around and ran. Will he ever be in trouble when Papa finds out!

Name _____

Answer the questions.

1. Create a graphic organizer that contains the important information from "The Liberty Bell."

2. Why do you think people named the bell the "Liberty Bell"?

   _____

   _____

3. In the fourth paragraph of "The Liberty Bell," what did the author mean by the phrase, *had to be retired*?

   _____

   _____

4. Explain why you think the author chose to title the second passage "Oops!" Use evidence from the passage in your answer.

   _____

   _____

5. What type of speech is "children should be seen and not heard"? What do you think this means?

   _____

   _____

6. What do you think Robert will do the next time Abigail wants to play hide-and-seek? Explain your thinking.

   _____

   _____

Name _____

7. Decide whether each passage is fiction or nonfiction. Label it accordingly. Provide evidence from both passages to support your answer.

	The Liberty Bell	**Oops!**
Type of passage		
Evidence		

8. Both passages have a bell as a central figure. Write a paragraph to explain the similarities and differences in the passages.

_____
_____
_____
_____
_____
_____
_____
_____
_____
_____
_____

The Orphan Trains

By the 1850s, New York City was thriving. Many people were flooding into its borders. One large part of the population was orphaned children. Some believe that over 30,000 children were homeless. They ranged in age from six to 18 years old. They lived on the streets or in slums.

Charles Loring Brace, founder of the Children's Aid Society, decided something had to be done. At the same time, many immigrants were trying to farm land throughout the West. Perhaps the children could escape a horrible life. They could be placed with families throughout America. Brace came up with the idea of sending the children out west on trains. He was hoping that this would benefit both parties. The families would get some much-needed help. The children would be taken in by farmers and treated like one of the family.

The children were given cardboard suitcases and placed on trains. Along the way, the trains made many stops. At each stop, the children would be cleaned up. They would leave the train and stand on a stage. Potential families would inspect the children. Then, they would decide whether to take them in.

Somewhere between 150,000 to 200,000 children rode the orphan trains. Although many children found good homes this way, not all did. Because of the orphan trains, many other reforms meant to help homeless children began.

Please?

Livin' on the streets wasn't no good. Never had any food, unless I fought for it. Nobody to trust neither. Scary. Dirty. Lonely. But, this train thing ain't no good neither. Got a little food, but not much. The lady in charge always yellin' at us to behave in one breath and then tellin' us we'll all get a real mom and dad in the next.

Little kids cryin' for their mamas. Every time we stop, they run a dirty rag over our faces and push us onto a stage. People lookin' at us like we're horses at auction. Touchin' my arms, talkin' about my muscles. Askin' me to open my mouth. That man's lucky I didn't use it to bite him!

Maddy, the girl next to me, has been cryin' all day. She had a brother, Luke. She clung to him, makin' sure nobody got near him. Sang to him at night to calm him down. Kinda liked that part.

Some family wanted him at our first stop today. Couldn't have no baby and so they picked him. Maddy begged to go too. Weren't havin' none of that. Put her back on that train pretty fast. They walked away cooin' to Luke, all lovey-dovey. Seemed like a nice family. Older son said they were. Don't know what it'd be like to have that. Being 12, I don't think it'll happen. Sometimes, though, at night when it's quiet, I dream about that. Maybe next stop I'll smile and say please.

Name _____

Answer the questions.

1. What is the main idea of "Orphan Trains"?

_____

_____

2. Which text structure did the author of "Orphan Trains" use?

    A. chronological/sequence   **B.** cause/effect

    C. problem/solution   **D.** compare/contrast

3. Do you think the orphan trains were a good idea? Explain your thinking.

_____

_____

_____

_____

4. Summarize "Please?" in your own words.

_____

_____

_____

5. Why do you think the author chose the title "Please?" Explain your thinking.

_____

_____

_____

6. Choose two words to describe the narrator of "Please?" and explain your thinking.

_____

_____

_____

Name _____

7. Use information from both passages to complete the organizer.

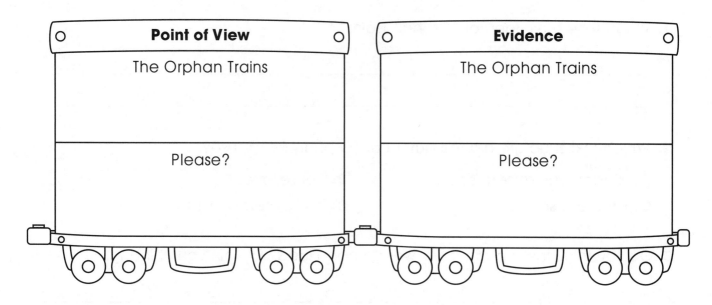

Point of View	Evidence
The Orphan Trains	The Orphan Trains
Please?	Please?

8. Write a dialogue to show a pretend conversation between Charles Loring Brace and the narrator of "Please?" Use information from both passages to shape the conversation. Think about each person's point of view.

_____

_____

_____

_____

_____

_____

_____

_____

_____

_____

_____

_____

_____

_____

An American Songwriter

Katherine Lee Bates was an English teacher at Wellesley College in Massachusetts. She was 33 years old in 1893 when she traveled by train to Colorado. Along the way, she saw many beautiful parts of America. She saw the World's Fair in Chicago, wheat fields in Kansas, and a majestic view from Pike's Peak. After all of this, she was inspired to put pen to paper and wrote this poem.

America the Beautiful

O beautiful for spacious skies,
    For amber waves of grain,
For purple mountain majesties
    Above the fruited plain!
      America! America!
    God shed His grace on thee
And crown thy good with brotherhood
    From sea to shining sea!

O beautiful for pilgrim feet,
    Whose stern, impassioned stress
A thoroughfare for freedom beat
    Across the wilderness!
      America! America!
    God mend thine every flaw,
Confirm thy soul in self-control,
    Thy liberty in law!

O beautiful for heroes proved
    In liberating strife,
Who more than self their country loved,
    And mercy more than life!
      America! America!
    May God thy gold refine
Till all success be nobleness,
    And every gain divine!

O beautiful for patriot dream
    That sees beyond the years
Thine alabaster cities gleam
    Undimmed by human tears!
      America! America!
    God shed His grace on thee,
And crown thy good with brotherhood
    From sea to shining sea!

Crossing Over

The Oregon City Times

October 15, 1863

One Family's Tale of Adventure

Oregon City, October 12.

William and Nell Jacob arrived just this week in the latest wagon train. They headed out just over five months ago with all of their belongings and their three children. When asked about the journey, Mr. Jacob shakes his head and sighs.

Little Laura, five years old, jumps up and down and squeals with delight as she tells me all about the friends she played with on the trail. Ten-year-old Elijah talks about the hard work of finding food for their family. Fourteen-year-old Benjamin discusses taking turns guarding the wagon train at night.

Mrs. Jacob quietly agrees that it was a long, difficult journey with many surprises along the way. "There was just so much beauty along with the uncertainty. Every day was something new. We saw long meadows full of blooming flowers, prairies full of tall grass as far as the eyes could see, rushing rivers so powerful that I thought we'd never make it across, stampeding buffalo like drums in my ears, lakes as still and clear as sheets of glass, and mountains so tall it would take weeks to cross them." Mr. Jacob added, "I will never forget the constant threat of attack by man or animal. That's what I remember."

Regardless of whom I spoke with, it was definitely a trip to remember and one that Mr. and Mrs. Jacob are not sure they would ever repeat!

Name _____

Answer the questions.

1. Ms. Bates, who wrote the poem "America the Beautiful," saw many beautiful sights. Find the line in the poem that she wrote about each sight and copy it below.

World's Fair in Chicago _____

_____

Wheat fields of Kansas _____

_____

Pike's Peak _____

_____

2. What do you think inspired Ms. Bates to write the third verse? Explain your thinking.

_____

_____

_____

3. The newspaper article uses figurative language to describe the trip. Find two examples and write them. Next to each example, explain what you think the author meant.

_____

_____

_____

_____

4. Why do you think everyone in the Jacob family had a different opinion about the journey? Explain your thinking.

_____

_____

_____

5. Ms. Bates and the Jacob family saw many of the same sights on their cross-country trips. List the physical features as well as the emotions they caused.

Physical feature	Emotion

6. Think about the journeys for Ms. Bates and the Jacob family. Write a short essay to discuss the similarities and differences in their points of view.

_____

_____

_____

_____

_____

_____

_____

_____

_____

_____

_____

_____

Babe Ruth

George Herman Ruth, Jr., was born in Baltimore, Maryland, on February 6, 1895. He was raised in a poor neighborhood. His parents had eight children, but six of them died as babies. By the time he was seven, George was constantly getting in trouble. He often drank alcohol, chewed tobacco, wandered the streets, and **harassed** the police. His parents finally sent him to a reform school for boys.

Ruth learned how to play baseball at the school. He was quite talented, and the owner of a local team, the Orioles, noticed him. Mr. Dunn, the owner, became his legal guardian so that George could sign a contract to play baseball professionally. His teammates called him "Dunn's new babe." This nickname stuck, and we know him today as Babe Ruth.

Ruth was called up to the Boston Red Sox fairly quickly, and he played for them for five years. The Sox then traded him to the New York Yankees. During his time with the Sox, he set a record for home runs. Throughout the following years, Babe continued to break his own records. He was never one to sit back and be content with what he had done. He was always working hard at the next record.

Ruth hit 714 home runs in his career, the third most in history. However, he struck out a total of 1,330 times. He once said, "Every single strike brings me closer to the next home run." Babe never once gave up.

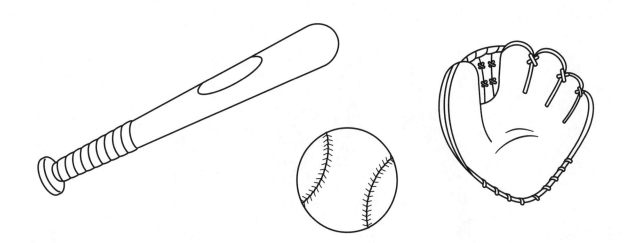

Shoot to Win, Ruby!

Hunter was the star of his college basketball team. Everyone wanted a piece of him after the games. All he cared about was finding his family. They came to every game. It pushed Hunter to play harder than anyone.

Hunter's sister, Ruby, followed him everywhere. She even played ball with him in the driveway. She said she would be a star just like him. When she was eight, she was in an accident and ended up in a wheelchair. For the first few years, the whole family was **devastated**. Then, with a change of heart, their parents began pushing Ruby to try new things. They wanted her to believe she could do anything anyone else could.

Hunter had seen something on TV that sparked an idea in his head: the Paralympic Games. This is a sports competition very much like the Olympics, but it is for people who have a range of physical disabilities. He especially liked that one of the events was Wheelchair Basketball. He began prodding Ruby to come out and shoot hoops with him.

"Your most important asset in basketball is your arms," he told her. She finally agreed, and they have been practicing daily since then.

It was hard work and, at first, Ruby missed far more baskets than she made. Hunter refused to let her give up. He told her about Babe Ruth's story and reminded her that Babe Ruth had more strikeouts than home runs. He pushed her harder than anyone, and Ruby became quite good. She even had a special chair she used for her practices.

Hunter and Ruby both caught the fever. The tryouts for the Paralympic team were coming up in less than six weeks, and Hunter couldn't wait to cheer her on!

Name _____

Answer the questions.

   I. Why do you think Babe Ruth got into so much trouble as a child?

_____

_____

   2. What made the difference for Babe Ruth?

_____

_____

   3. What does the word **harassed** mean as used in "Babe Ruth"?

     A. helped   **B.** teased

     C. bothered   **D.** ignored

   4. What is the author's purpose in "Shoot to Win, Ruby"?

_____

_____

   5. What is the main idea of "Shoot to Win, Ruby"?

_____

_____

   6. Which details support the main idea of "Shoot to Win, Ruby"?

_____

_____

_____

   7. What does the word **devastated** mean as used in "Shoot to Win, Ruby"?

     A. extremely upset   **B.** extremely happy

     C. very tired   **D.** very energetic

Name _____

8. Things happen in lives that cause people to respond in either good or bad ways. This is when people's character shows. Think about the events in both passages and complete the organizer.

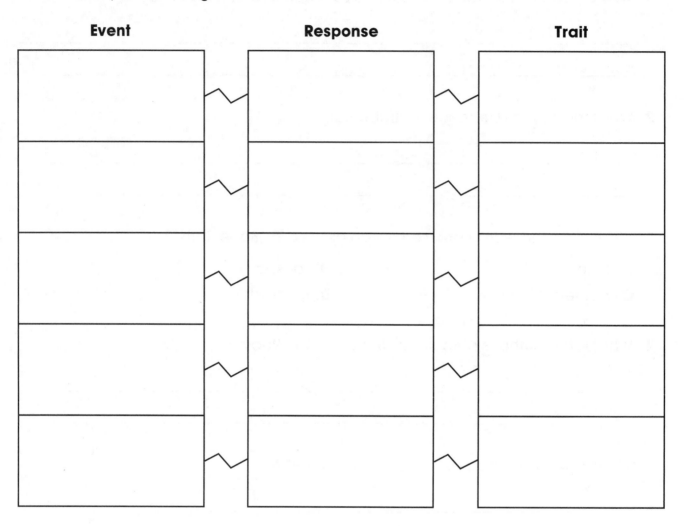

Event	Response	Trait

9. Think about the main characters in both passages. Why do you think Hunter used Babe Ruth as an example for Ruby? How did this help? Provide evidence from both passages to support your thinking.

_____

_____

_____

_____

_____

Cork for All Reasons

Have your parents ever told you, "Money doesn't grow on trees"? This is an idiom that means an **abundance** of money is not just laying around for us to pick up anytime we want. One interesting thing that does grow on trees, though, is cork.

Most trees have a layer of cork cambium close to the outer layer of bark. It is a protective layer that is water, rot, and fire resistant. In addition, termites and gas cannot get through it. As these cork cambium cells die, they move to the outside layer and become the bark that we see.

The cork oak is a special tree that grows mainly near the Mediterranean Sea. The area has a lot of sunshine, very little rain, and high humidity. This allows a thicker layer of cork to grow. This thick layer of cork protects the tree from the harsh environment. The cork oak is the main source of cork products used all over the world.

After a cork oak is 25 years old, the bark can be harvested. Once the cork is harvested the first time, the bark can only be stripped every eight to 14 years. The bark is then used to make many different products. Some people use the cork for flooring. Others place corkboards in their homes, offices, or schools and use them to post messages, fun quotes, or photos. The most common use, however, are as bottle stoppers.

Cork has many uses and is a popular product in many places around the world. Its harvest also provides many jobs. Over 100,000 people have jobs harvesting cork. In fact, some entire communities in Africa depend on the wages of cork harvesting.

Depending on how you look at it, maybe money does grow on trees!

A Surprising Tree

Have you ever had a bad cold and one of your parents rubbed some menthol under your nose or on your chest to help you breathe? If so, that medicine was made from a eucalyptus tree.

The eucalyptus tree is found mainly in Australia. It can be from 33 to 200 feet (10 to 60 m) tall when fully grown. It has a long, straight trunk and is covered in rough bark. Because it is an evergreen, it does not lose its leaves. The leaves are covered in oil glands, which have many uses.

Eucalyptus leaves are an important part of a koala's diet. The leaves can be **toxic** if a large amount is eaten, so koalas smell them to determine when and how much to eat.

Although eucalyptus leaves are a favorite of koalas, some of their other uses may surprise you! They are the most common source of pulp, which is used in papermaking. The oil from the leaves is used in medicines, sweets, cough drops, and toothpaste. The nectar can be made into honey. And, a traditional Australian musical instrument called the didgeridoo is made from eucalyptus tree wood.

The eucalyptus tree is also known as the gum tree. Do you remember a childhood song that begins, "Kookaburra sits in the old gum tree"? The song uses the eucalyptus tree's common name. The kookaburra is a large bird with a loud, cackling birdcall. The kookaburra makes its home in the eucalyptus forest of eastern Australia.

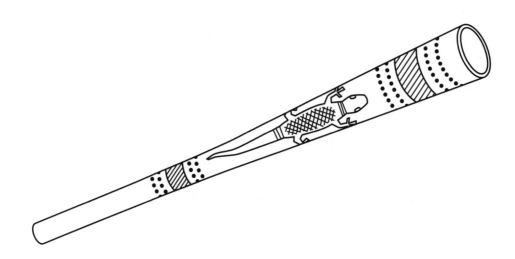

Name _____

Answer the questions.

1. What is the main idea of "Cork for All Reasons"?

   A. The bark of a cork tree helps protect it.

   B. Cork trees are very strong.

   C. A cork tree has many uses.

   D. Cork bottle stoppers are made from cork trees.

2. Which statement from the passage best supports the main idea?

   A. One interesting thing that does grow on trees, though, is cork.

   B. The cork oak is a special tree that grows mainly near the Mediterranean Sea.

   C. After a cork oak is 25 years old, the bark can be harvested.

   D. The bark is then used to make many different products.

3. According to "A Surprising Tree," which part of the eucalyptus tree is the most useful?

   A. the trunk   **B.** the leaves   **C.** the menthol   **D.** the bark

4. What does the word **toxic** mean as used in "A Surprising Tree"?

   A. harmful   **B.** helpful   **C.** filling   **D.** nutritious

5. What does the word **abundance** mean as used in "Cork for All Reasons"?

   A. plenty   **B.** lack   **C.** need   **D.** scarcity

6. If eucalyptus leaves can be toxic for koalas when they eat large amounts, why do you think people are able to use eucalyptus in many everyday products?

   _____

   _____

7. What is the main idea of "A Surprising Tree"?

   _____

   _____

Name _____

8. Use the information from both passages to complete the graphic organizer.

Cork Oak   **Eucalyptus**

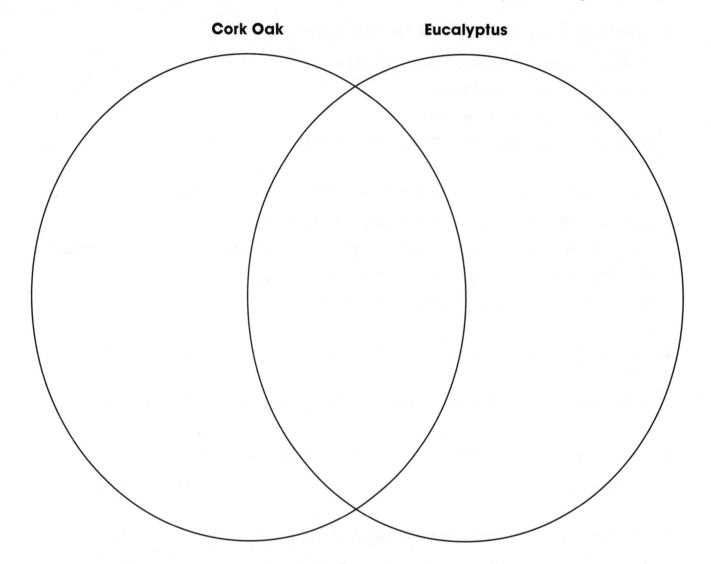

9. Use the information from the Venn diagram to write a summary about the similarities and differences between the cork oak and the eucalyptus tree.

_____

_____

_____

_____

_____

_____

_____

A Long, Cold Walk

When was the last time you saw a person using a phone while driving? It was probably the last time you were in a car. The National Safety Council estimates that 1.6 million accidents happen each year because of the use of cell phones. Over 330,000 people are injured in these accidents. Unfortunately for the Hill family, this is exactly what happened in 2002.

The Hill family had spent Thanksgiving Day with their family in Colorado. The three children changed into their pajamas, said good-bye, and then climbed into the family truck for the ride home. At some point, the mother's cell phone rang. As she reached over to answer it, she lost control of her truck. She couldn't gain control, and the truck ended up rolling over five times before it came to a stop.

All three children were in the back seat. Fortunately, all three were strapped in seatbelts or car seats and were fine. The oldest, seven-year-old Titus, checked on his two siblings. He then realized his mother had been thrown from the truck and was unconscious, lying in the snow. He immediately went to get help. He walked barefoot through the snow for half a mile. He found some dairy workers on a farm who called paramedics. Because of Titus's quick thinking, his mom was rescued.

The Hill family is very fortunate that Titus acted quickly. Not all families in accidents are as lucky. If someone you are riding with tries to pick up a cell phone, share the story of the Hill family. Maybe that will make the person think twice. Also, you may wish to remind drivers that in many states, it is against the law to talk on handheld devices while driving.

The Big, Yellow Bus

How do you get to school each day? If you ride the bus, you are not alone. Over 25 million students use this form of transportation each morning. Because it is such a normal part of the day, most students do not even pay much attention to their surroundings. They talk to friends, listen to music, read books, do homework, or just stare out the window. Luckily for one school bus, seventh-grader Jeremy Wuitschick was paying close attention.

On an April morning in 2012, Jeremy boarded the bus in Milton, Washington, and sat in his seat, just a few rows from the front of the bus. He looked up and noticed the bus driver slump down in his seat. The bus continued moving forward, but the driver's hands were no longer on the wheel. The bus driver had fainted. At that instant, no one was steering the bus!

Jeremy leaped out of his seat and ran to the front of the bus. He grabbed the steering wheel. He steered the bus to the side of the road, but he could not reach the pedals. Using quick thinking, he yanked the keys out of the ignition. He said later that he remembered reading about such a situation in a superhero book, where someone was able to stop a runaway bus by pulling the keys from the ignition.

This time, Jeremy was the superhero. The bus came to a stop. Some of the other kids on the bus called 911 for help. One of Jeremy's classmates, seventh-grader Johnny Wood, had studied CPR. He became a hero himself by performing CPR on the bus driver until help could arrive.

Thanks to Jeremy's quick thinking and actions, every student on the bus was kept safe. And, thanks to Johnny, so was the bus driver!

Name _____

Answer the questions.

1. What is the main idea of the first paragraph of "A Long, Cold Walk"?

   _____

   _____

2. What details does the author use to support this idea?

   _____

   _____

3. What is the main idea of the first paragraph of "The Big, Yellow Bus"?

   _____

   _____

4. What details does the author use to support this idea?

   _____

   _____

5. Why do you think the author of "A Long, Cold Walk" included the information about cell phones and accidents?

   _____

   _____

6. Why do you think the author of "The Big, Yellow Bus" included the information about the number of students riding buses to school each day?

   _____

   _____

7. Use the graphic organizer to compare and contrast the two passages.

Jeremy   **Titus**

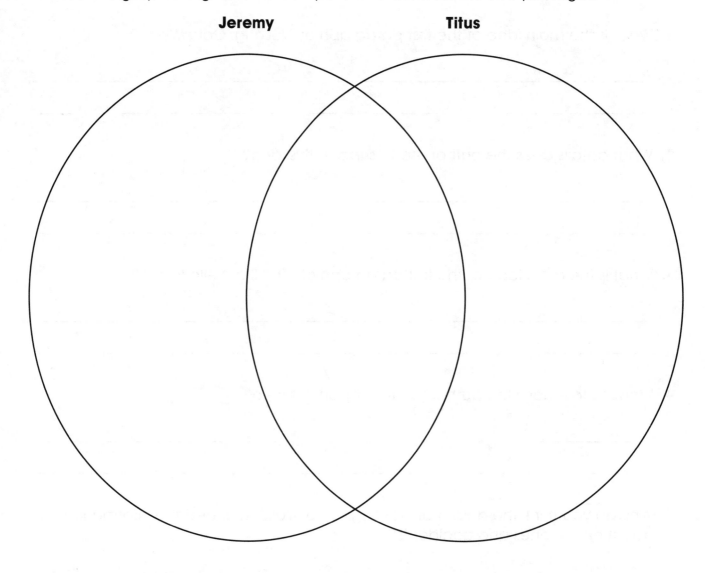

8. Think about Titus, Jeremy, and Johnny. Choose at least three words to describe the characteristics they have in common. Use evidence from both passages to support your choices.

_____

_____

_____

_____

_____

_____

Exercise Matters

Recess and PE may be most kids' favorite times of the school day. This is because these times do not involve reading, writing, or arithmetic! However, some might argue that they are the favorite times of the school day for most doctors as well.

It is now believed that more than one in three children are overweight. This is **alarming** to health professionals. It is also why recess and PE are getting a lot of press these days. They are the only times of day that students are not sitting still. Unfortunately, not all students have recess or PE daily. This makes it important for children to get exercise at home as well.

Exercise can come in many forms: stretching, yoga, walking, running, biking, tennis, swimming, team sports, bowling, jumping rope, and even flying a kite. The possibilities are endless, and so are the benefits.

Exercise improves health in many ways. It helps prevent many diseases and helps control weight. It also strengthens the heart and lungs. People who exercise live about seven years longer than those who do not. With benefits like that, you might be tempted to ask for more recess!

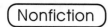

Work Your Body to Improve Your Mind

Many people exercise to help improve their bodies' health. However, recent studies show that exercise has many benefits that improve people's minds as well. And, you do not have to run a marathon or win a tournament to get the benefits!

Exercise has been proven to reduce stress. If you are worried about a book report or a big game coming up, shoot a few baskets. The effort will help your brain deal with the worry.

Exercise can make you happier. Are you having a bad week? Did you have a disagreement with a friend? Are you feeling down? Go for a bike ride and let the endorphins **boost** your mood.

Physical activity can help give you added brainpower. It aids in new learning. It also helps improve memory. Do you have a big test coming up? Go for a run before studying. You will be surprised at how much more you can learn.

Regular exercise can help you sleep better. Is counting sheep not working? Try a daily dose of soccer. Just be sure it is a few hours before bedtime. When your body temperature returns to normal, it signals your brain that it is time for sleep.

Finally, exercise helps with creativity. Are you having a difficult time writing that book report? Jump rope with some friends and then try again.

Exercise: It's not just for your health anymore!

Name _____

Answer the questions.

1. What does the word **alarming** mean as used in "Exercise Matters"?

   A. disturbing   **B.** restful   **C.** noisy   **D.** helpful

2. Why do you think the author chose the title "Exercise Matters"?

   _____

   _____

3. What would be another good title for "Exercise Matters"? Use evidence from the passage to support your thinking.

   _____

   _____

4. What does the word **boost** mean as used in "Work Your Body to Improve Your Mind"?

   A. change   **B.** lower   **C.** improve   **D.** end

5. Why do you think the author ended the passage with, "Exercise: It's not just for your health anymore!"?

   _____

   _____

   _____

6. What was the author's purpose for writing "Recess, Anyone?"?

   _____

   _____

   _____

   _____

   _____

   _____

Name _____

7. Think about both articles. Determine one main idea that would fit both. List it in the chart below and then fill in the details from each passage that support the main idea.

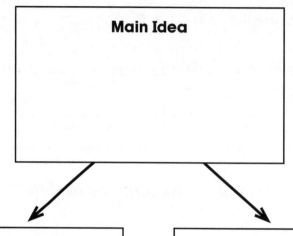

Main Idea

Details: Exercise Matters

Details: Work Your Body to Improve Your Mind

8. Using information from the chart, write a letter to your teacher asking him or her to give you more recess. Be sure to support all of your thinking with evidence.

_____

_____

_____

_____

_____

_____

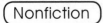

Centuries-Old Mystery

In 1587, 117 men and women left England headed to the "New World." In July, they landed at Roanoke Island, Virginia. Roanoke Island is one of a chain of barrier islands off the coast of North Carolina that is today called the Outer Banks.

Although many think Plymouth is where America began, Roanoke was truly the first American settlement. John White was the governor of this small colony. There were many hardships, but more than 100 settlers made Roanoke their home.

One thing many people complained about was the lack of tools and supplies. So, White went back to England to get these items. Unfortunately, this trip took three years. When White returned, he was shocked. The settlement was **deserted**. The fort was destroyed and the homes were abandoned. The colony was surrounded by overgrown bush.

As he investigated further, he found a single word, "CROATOAN," carved into the side of a large fence. As luck would have it, a hurricane arose and damaged White's ship. This forced him to return to England again. The fate of the colony haunted White until the day he died. What had happened to his family and the rest of the colonists? He never found out.

There are many theories about what might have happened. Did the colonists leave to settle somewhere else? Were they killed by American Indians or by disease? Had a storm, such as a hurricane, blown through and destroyed everything and everyone? Or, had they left to join the friendly Native Americans who lived on the nearby island of Croatoan?

Unfortunately, this is one mystery that may never be solved. The only thing we know for sure is that the entire settlement disappeared, never to be heard from again. Today, the Roanoke Colony is also known as the "Lost Colony."

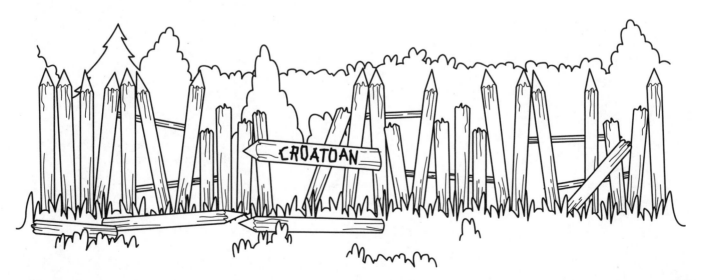

The Green Children of Woolpit

During the 12th century in the village of Woolpit, England, two children appeared in a field. Both the boy and the girl had skin that was tinted green. They were dressed in clothing made of an unknown material and spoke in an unusual language no one could understand. The workers took the children into the village where a local family took care of them.

Although they appeared to be starving, the children refused food. Much later, some villagers brought by some beans. The children **devoured** them. They ate only beans for months until they developed a taste for bread.

The brother eventually became sick and died, but the sister remained alive. Her skin lost its green tint over time and she learned to speak English. She explained that she and her brother had been raised in a distant land without sun and where everyone was green. One day, while watching their father's flock, they found a cave. They went into it and walked a long way until they came out on the other side, which was the field where they were discovered.

Over the years, many theories have developed. Were the children sick with a disease that changed the color of their skin? Was the cave a mine shaft that ended near the field? Did they fall from heaven? Was it possible they were aliens from another planet who somehow found their way to Earth?

No one knows the answer and it is doubtful now that anyone ever will. It is really anyone's guess, since there are no survivors of that time. What do you think?

Name _____

Answer the questions.

1. What does the word **deserted** mean as used in "Centuries-Old Mystery"?

    A. resembling a large area of sand without much rain

    B. tasting like something sweet

    C. in very bad shape

    D. empty, with no one around

2. What is the main idea of "Centuries-Old Mystery"?

    _____

    _____

3. List at least three details which support the main idea.

    _____

    _____

4. What was the author's purpose for writing "The Green Children of Woolpit"?

    _____

    _____

5. How are both passages similar?

    _____

    _____

6. How are both passages different?

    _____

    _____

7. What does the word **devoured** mean as used in "The Green Children of Woolpit"?

    A. threw away   **B.** ate quickly   **C.** destroyed   **D.** returned

Name _____

8. List at least two theories mentioned in each passage. List evidence from the passages to support each theory.

Theory	Evidence

9. Think about both passages and the way the authors ended them. How are the endings similar? Why do you think the authors chose to end them in this way? What do you think the authors hoped the reader would do?

_____

_____

_____

_____

_____

Light the Night

The first lighthouses date back to more than 2,800 years ago. The forerunners of the first lighthouses were bonfires set on hilltops. They were lit to guide seamen safely to shore. The first modern lighthouses were built in about 1700. At that time, fires were still being used. It was not until the 1800s that oil, gas, and electric lamps were used instead.

Keeping a fire burning was a hard job. Because of this, the original "lighthouses" were only used when boats were returning to shore. As easier lighting methods were developed, it became more common for lighthouses to operate as continual beacons for sailors.

In addition to better lighting, many other improvements have been made over the years. In 1777, one lighthouse began using mirrors as a way to make the light more intense. The downside to this was that the beam of light only shot out in one direction. This is when the revolving light came into use. At first, **mariners** did not like this. They were used to guiding their boats based on a single, solid light. Over time, they adapted and grew to like the rotating beam. Today, many lighthouses are known by the rhythm of their lights.

Another important feature of lighthouses is the daymark. During the day, the lights cannot be seen. Because of this, lighthouses must be painted to stand out in contrast to their surroundings. It allows sailors to easily spot them both day and night. Shore lighthouses are usually painted white for this reason.

Over time, others improve upon the design of most inventions. Fortunately for sailors, this has been the case with lighthouses. Who knows how many thousands of lives have been saved through the years due to the invention of the lighthouse?

Keep the Light Burning, Abbie

Sixteen-year-old Abbie Burgess lived with her parents off the coast of Maine. Her mother was an invalid and could not help with anything, so Abbie took care of her younger siblings. Her father was the lighthouse keeper. She learned how to keep the light burning so that her father could fish for lobsters to sell.

One January day in 1856, Abbie's father went to the mainland to buy food and oil. Her brother was out fishing. The wind changed and a ferocious storm, a nor'easter, blew in. Realizing the danger, Abbie moved the family into the lighthouse.

The waves increased and washed away anything that was not secured. Abbie knew that their only hope was the strength and safety of the lighthouse. However, Abbie worried about their hens and decided to try to rescue them. She ran outside when the waves were receding and was able to rescue all but one. She had barely made it back inside when the worst waves yet came and washed away the rest of their house. But, the lighthouse still stood.

Abbie had to complete not only her chores, but her father's as well. Most importantly, she had to keep the oil lit in the lighthouse to protect any boats sailing by. Because of the weather and the waves, her father could not land safely. For 21 straight days, Abbie took care of all of the chores, her family, and the lighthouse without any help.

Later, Abbie wrote a letter to a friend telling her what had happened. She described it this way: "I cannot think you would enjoy remaining here any great length of time for the sea is never still, and when agitated, its roar shuts out every other sound, even drowning our voices."

Name _____

Answer the questions.

1. List three aspects of a lighthouse and how this helps seamen.

Aspect	Benefit

2. What does the word **mariner** mean as used in "Light the Night"?

   A. boats   **B.** seaman

   C. lighthouse keepers   **D.** visitors

3. What do you think the author of "Light the Night" meant when she wrote, "Today, many lighthouses are known by the rhythm of their lights"?

   _____

   _____

4. Use two words to describe Abbie Burgess. Provide evidence from the passage for each word.

   _____

   _____

5. Which text structure did the author use in "Keep the Fire Burning, Abbie"?

   A. description   **B.** cause/effect

   C. compare/contrast   **D.** directions

6. Use your own words to state what Abbie meant when she said, ". . . for the sea is never still, and when agitated, its roar shuts out every other sound, even drowning our voices."

   _____

   _____

Name _____

7. Lighthouses play a role in both passages. Think about whether they play the role of *main* or *supporting* character and the evidence in the passage that proves this. Fill in the organizer below with your thoughts.

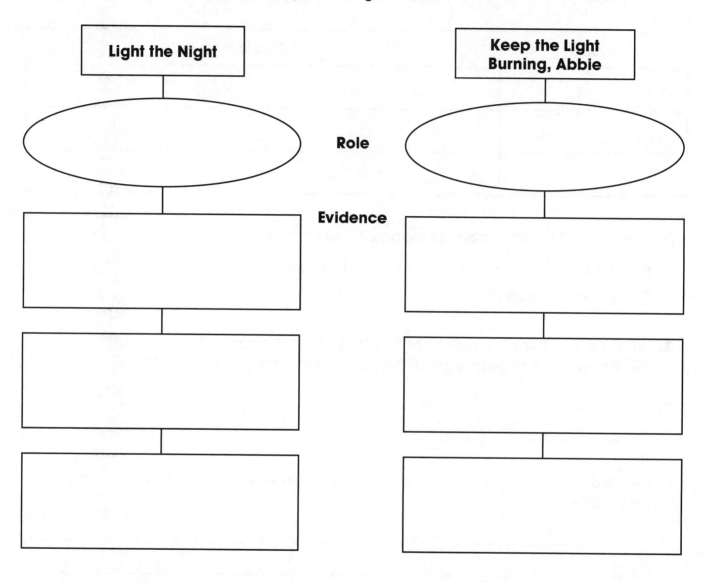

8. Use what you learned from "Light the Night" to write about what might have happened had Abbie lived during the 1600s.

_____

_____

_____

_____

_____

_____

What Was That?

Benjamin Franklin was an intelligent man. He constantly thought about how things worked. In the 1740s, electricity was not common like it is today. People used it for magic tricks by creating sparks. It was not a useful tool at all.

Franklin was curious about electricity and noticed that it was similar to lightning in many ways. They were both very loud, created light, were attracted to metal, and smelled much the same. After observing them for some time, he wondered if they were the same thing.

In order to prove his theory, Franklin needed to find something tall. There were no hills or tall buildings in Philadelphia, so he puzzled about another plan. How could he get up in the sky without a hill or building? Franklin decided to build a kite and try it that way. He used a silk handkerchief, two sticks, and a string. He flew the kite into the sky during a thunderstorm to see what happened. It worked! He proved that electricity and lightning are the same thing!

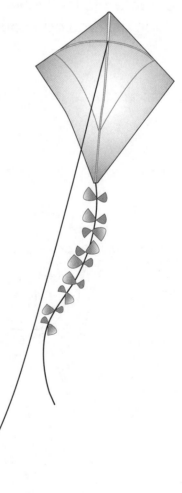

Then, Franklin wanted to use this knowledge to help people. He knew many buildings burned down because of lightning. He also knew that lightning struck the highest point of a building. So, he invented a lightning rod. This way, the lightning would hit the lightning rod and the electricity would travel down into the ground without hurting anyone.

A Powerful Force

Lightning is one of the most powerful forces on earth. It is a giant charge of electricity. Lightning can travel over 5 miles (8 km) and can have 100 million to 100 billion electrical volts. Scientists believe that Earth is struck by 100 lightning bolts every single second!

During storms, ice particles in clouds bounce around. They run into each other. The positively charged electrical crystals go to the top of the cloud. The negative ones float to the bottom. In a storm, an object on the ground has a positive charge. Because of this, the negative crystals are drawn to it. This causes lightning.

Lightning is hotter than the sun. It can split large trees in half. Many buildings are damaged by lightning each year. Most now have some form of lightning rod in order to help prevent this. About 22,000 forest fires are started by lightning each year. And, over 300 people are struck by lightning annually in the United States alone.

What can you do? Stay inside during a storm. Keep away from water. Stay off the phone. If it is not possible to get inside, find some kind of shelter immediately. Since lightning is attracted to the highest point, hiding under a tree is not a good idea. Do not go back outside until you can count to 30 between a lightning strike and the thunder.

Name _____

Answer the questions.

  1. What was the author's purpose in writing "What Was That?"?

    _____

    _____

  2. How does the author support the statement, "Benjamin Franklin was an intelligent man"? Provide at least three pieces of evidence from the passage.

    _____

    _____

    _____

  3. How do you think Benjamin Franklin's discovery has helped us today?

    _____

    _____

  4. What was the author's purpose in writing "A Powerful Force"?

    _____

    _____

  5. How does the author best support the statement, "Lightning is one of the most powerful forces on earth"?

    A. It can travel over 5 miles (8 km) and contains at least 100 million electrical volts.

    B. Scientists believe that Earth is struck by 100 lightning bolts every single second!

    C. Many buildings are damaged by lightning each year.

    D. It is a giant charge of electricity.

  6. What would be another good title for "A Powerful Force"? Explain your thinking.

    _____

    _____

    _____

Name _____

7. Think about how lightning plays a central role in both passages. Complete the following organizer.

	What Was That?	**A Powerful Force**
Main Idea		
Supporting Details		

8. Do you think Benjamin Franklin would have conducted his experiment if he had read "A Powerful Force"? Use evidence from both passages to support your opinion.

_____

_____

_____

_____

_____

_____

_____

_____

_____

_____

Trail of Tears

In 1830, the US government, led by President Andrew Jackson, passed the Indian Removal Act. This allowed the government to force all American Indians east of the Mississippi River to move to other locations. The settlers in those areas wanted the land for themselves. American Indians fought this act. They took their fight all the way to the Supreme Court, the highest court in the land. The court ruled in their favor. President Jackson ignored the court and moved forward with his plans.

In 1838, President Martin Van Buren sent 7,000 soldiers to force 15,000 Cherokee to move. They left their homes with very few possessions. What they left behind, the soldiers and settlers kept for themselves. The Cherokee began their journey during the summer. They walked west for over 1,000 miles (1,609 km). Many times, the land was not clear, so the American Indian men on the trek had to chop down the trees in order to continue moving. They had to cross mountains and rough waters. They walked all the way to Oklahoma, then called Indian Territory.

The walk was brutal. Very little food or water was available along the way. They walked through winter, and it was very cold. Many got sick. Because of these hardships, over 4,000 died. The American Indians called this forced walk *Nunahi-Duna-Dlo-Hilu-I* or "Trail Where They Cried." Today, we call it the Trail of Tears. In all, over 1,000,000 American Indians from five tribes were forced to move.

This journey was a devastating time for the Cherokee and a sad part of American history. Today, what was once called Indian Territory is the state of Oklahoma.

The Underground Railroad

Between the years of 1810 and 1850, a secret "railroad" was helping to free southern slaves. This was called the Underground Railroad. Believe it or not, it was neither underground nor a railroad. It was called this because many railroad terms were used to describe what was happening.

At this time in American history, there were over 1.2 million slaves. Many people did not agree with this. Some of them decided to do something about it. First, though, the slaves had to escape their masters. Once they did, they could try to make their way to a "station." This was a house or building where they could rest and eat. The people who ran these were called "stationmasters." From here, a "conductor" would help lead the escaped slaves to the next station.

Most of this happened at night. They would usually travel 10 to 20 miles (16.1 to 32.2 km) before stopping to rest. Many people donated money to help provide food, clothes, and transportation to these slaves. In addition, some would even help provide jobs.

Levi Coffin was one of the most daring and famous members of the Railroad. He was a businessman. He operated part of the railroad in Ohio and Indiana. In fact, his house is often called the "Grand Central Station of the Underground Railroad." He helped free over 3,000 slaves. Without him, and others like him, many slaves would have never reached freedom. In all, it is believed that over 100,000 slaves were freed this way.

Answer the questions.

1. Why is "Trail of Tears" a good description of what happened to the American Indians?

   _____

   _____

2. Think about "Trail of Tears." What is the author's point of view? Provide evidence from the passage to support your answer.

   _____

   _____

3. What are two arguments the Cherokee could have used when the militia showed up to force them to leave? Use the passage for support.

   _____

   _____

4. What is the author's message in "The Underground Railroad"?

   _____

   _____

5. Think of another name that could have been given to the Underground Railroad. Why would this have been a good name?

   _____

   _____

6. Most of the travel took place at night. Why do you think this was the case? What issues would this have caused?

   _____

   _____

   _____

Name _____

7. Trails and travel play a central role in both passages. Think about the purpose these trails played as you complete the chart below.

	Trail of Tears	**Underground Railroad**
Purpose of Trails and Travel		
Supporting Evidence		

8. Use the information from the chart above to help you write about the similarities and differences in the Trail of Tears and the Underground Railroad.

_____

_____

_____

_____

_____

_____

_____

_____

_____

_____

Jordan Spieth, Golfer Extraordinaire

Jordan Spieth was born in Dallas, Texas, on July 27, 1993. His parents, Shawn and Chris, were both athletes. He has two younger siblings. He was always looking after them. Jordan played baseball, basketball, football, golf, and soccer as he was growing up. He eventually chose golf as his sport of choice. He has proven that this was one of the best decisions of his life!

When Jordan was nine years old, he took out the family mower. He made a section of his lawn as low as he could so that he might practice his putting. It was then that his parents joined a golf club. They wanted him to have a true course to practice on.

Jordan's parents have said that he was a typical boy growing up—he goofed off with his friends and got in trouble. However, he worked hard at school. He made the honor roll every single semester. He went on to college but dropped out after less than one year in order to **pursue** his love of golf.

He began playing on the pro tour in 2013. He finished in the Top 10 in his first two events. He continued to play well and won his first PGA (Professional Golf Association) title at 19, becoming the youngest winner since 1931. He was named Rookie of the Year and has played professional golf ever since.

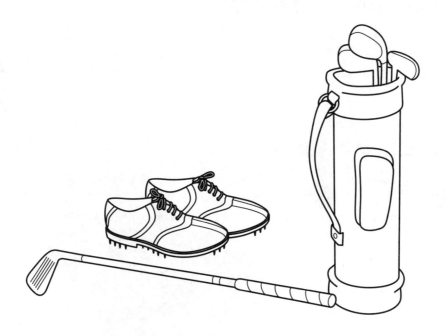

Adam Levine, Music Man

Adam Noah Levine was born on March 18, 1979, in Los Angeles, California. His parents, Patsy and Fredric, had four other children. Adam and some of his junior high friends formed a band, Kara's Flowers. He originally played guitar. Since then he has branched out and plays many other instruments. He has been seen playing keyboards, piano, accordion, drums, and many different forms of guitar.

Kara's Flowers had their first gig at a high school dance. Adam was so shy that he had to face the back of the stage. He went to a private high school. After this he went on to college in New York City. He dropped out of college after only one semester and went back home to Los Angeles. He joined up with his old band mates. They added one more band member and became Maroon 5.

In New York, Adam had his heart broken when his girlfriend broke up with him. He wanted something positive to come out of it. Because of this, he wrote lots of songs about his former girlfriend. They were the songs Maroon 5 recorded on their first album. The album became a huge success! The band won a Grammy Award for best new artist in 2004.

Adam has openly stated that he has been diagnosed with ADHD (Attention Deficit Hyperactivity Disorder). Many believe that this has been a factor in his learning so many different instruments and working such long hours. No one can deny the success of his career. He is definitely one talented music man!

Name _____

Answer the questions.

1. How does the author of "Jordan Spieth, Golfer Extraordinaire" best support the statement, "He has proven that this was one of the best decisions of his life!"?

   A. He eventually chose golf as his sport of choice.

   B. He made a section of his lawn as low as he could so that he might practice putting.

   C. He dropped out of college after less than one year in order to pursue golf.

   D. He continued to play well and won his first PGA (Professional Golf Association) title at 19, becoming the youngest winner since 1931.

2. What does the word **pursue** mean as used in "Jordan Spieth, Golfer Extraordinaire"?

   A. give up   B. go after   C. support   D. begin

3. What do you think would have happened if Jordan's parents had not joined a golf club? Support your thinking.

   _____

   _____

4. How does the author of "Adam Levine, Music Man" best support the statement, "He is definitely one talented music man!"?

   A. He has been seen playing keyboards, piano, accordion, drums, and many different forms of guitar.

   B. They added one more band member and became Maroon 5.

   C. They were the songs Maroon 5 recorded on their first album.

   D. The band won a Grammy Award for best new artist in 2004.

5. There is an idiom in "Adam Levine, Music Man." Find it, write it, and tell what it really means.

   _____

   _____

   _____

   _____

Name _____

6. Think about both Jordan Spieth and Adam Levine. What are some things that they have in common? What are some of their differences? Fill out the organizer.

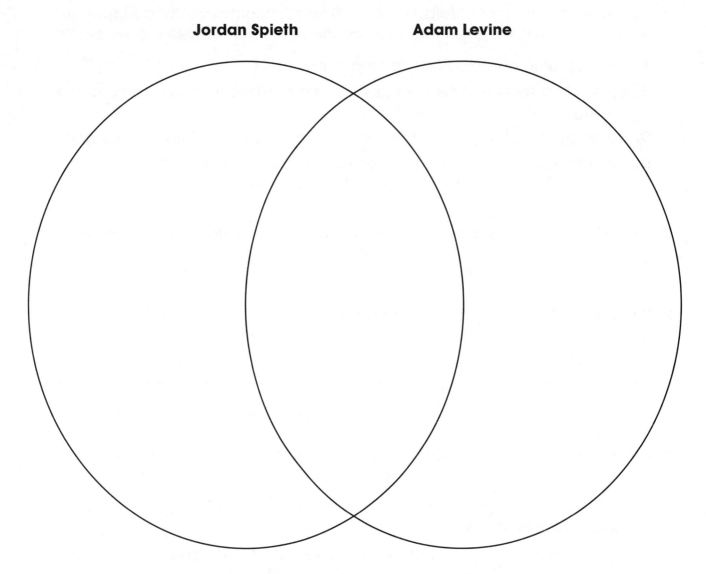

Jordan Spieth   **Adam Levine**

7. Think about what it takes to become successful at something. Write a paragraph about the character traits that both Jordan Spieth and Adam Levine have that helped make them successful. Support your thinking with text evidence.

_____

_____

_____

_____

_____

_____

After Apple-Picking
by Robert Frost

My long two-pointed ladder's sticking
through a tree

Toward heaven still,

And there's a barrel that I didn't fill

Beside it, and there may be two or three

Apples I didn't pick upon some bough.

But I am done with apple-picking now.

Essence of winter sleep is on the night,

The scent of apples: I am drowsing off.

I cannot rub the strangeness from my
sight

I got from looking through a pane of glass

I skimmed this morning from the drinking
trough

And held against the world of hoary
grass.

It melted, and I let it fall and break.

But I was well

Upon my way to sleep before it fell,

And I could tell

What form my dreaming was about to
take.

Magnified apples appear and disappear,

Stem end and blossom end,

And every fleck of russet showing clear.

My instep arch not only keeps the ache,

It keeps the pressure of a ladder-round.

I feel the ladder sway as the boughs bend.

And I keep hearing from the cellar bin

The rumbling sound

Of load on load of apples coming in.

For I have had too much

Of apple-picking: I am overtired

Of the great harvest I myself desired.

There were ten thousand thousand fruit to
touch,

Cherish in hand, lift down, and not let fall.

For all

That struck the earth,

No matter if not bruised or spiked with
stubble,

Went surely to the cider-apple heap

As of no worth.

One can see what will trouble

This sleep of mine, whatever sleep it is.

Were he not gone,

The woodchuck could say whether it's
like his

Long sleep, as I describe its coming on,

Or just some human sleep.

Dear Diary

October 12, 1873

Dear Diary,

I can barely keep my eyes open. It has been a long day that began before the sun even rose. Papa woke me up early to begin the chores. Because it is harvest time, he and the boys are working all day in the fields. This leaves me to take care of all the chores and cooking, as Mama is in bed with a fever.

I had barely finished cooking and cleaning up breakfast before the cows were loudly calling me to milk them. Of course, one of them kicked the pail over and I lost some of the milk. After finishing that I had to go straight to the barn to clean it out and take care of feeding the chickens. At least there were plenty of eggs this morning and Natalie is old enough to help with them!

I made a pail full of cheese and biscuits and took it out in the fields to Pa and the boys. No sooner had I finished that than I had to begin the laundry. I had barely finished supper when the boys came running in. After feeding everyone and getting Natalie in bed, I asked for a candle so I could write to you. I pray Mama is better soon.

Good night,

Sara

Name _____

Answer the questions.

1. Based upon "After Apple-Picking," what did the narrator skim from the water trough?

   A. a window pane   **B.** an apple

   C. a piece of ice   **D.** a child's toy

2. What is the main idea of "After Apple-Picking"?

   A. Apple picking is important.

   B. Apple picking is tiring work.

   C. The narrator had to be careful when picking apples.

   D. The narrator is falling asleep.

3. Which statement from "After Apple-Picking" best supports the main idea?

   A. The scent of apples: I am drowsing off

   B. There were ten thousand thousand fruit to touch

   C. My long two-pointed ladder's sticking through a tree toward heaven still

   D. For I have had too much of apple-picking: I am overtired

4. Based upon the diary entry, why did Sara have to do so many chores?

   A. Papa was taking care of the harvest.

   B. Natalie is still too young.

   C. Mama is sick with a fever.

   D. The boys are in the fields working.

5. Which chore was not Sara's responsibility?

   A. gathering the eggs   **B.** helping with the harvest

   C. milking the cows   **D.** cooking supper

6. How are both narrators similar?

   _____

   _____

   _____

Name _____

7. How are both narrators different?

_____

_____

8. Choose two character traits that would describe both narrators. Use words from each passage as evidence to support your thinking.

Character Trait	After Apple-Picking	Dear Diary
◯		
◯		

9. Write another diary entry pretending to be the narrator from "After Apple-Picking." Use words from the poem to guide your entry.

_____

_____

_____

_____

_____

_____

_____

_____

The Crow and the Pitcher
by Aesop (adapted)

Crow, half-dead with thirst, came upon a pitcher that had once been full of water. But, when Crow put his beak into the mouth of the pitcher, he found that only very little water was left in it and that he could not reach far enough down to get at it. He tried and he tried, but at last had to give up in despair.

Suddenly, a thought came to him, and he took a pebble and dropped it into the pitcher. Then, he took another pebble and dropped it into the pitcher. He took another pebble and dropped that into the pitcher. Once again, he took another pebble and dropped it into the pitcher. He took another pebble and dropped that into the pitcher. Again, he took another pebble and dropped that into the pitcher. He continued doing this for some time.

At last, Crow saw the water mount up near him, and after casting in a few more pebbles, he was able to quench his thirst and save his life.

Do I Have To?

Jordan opened the door, dropped her backpack, and dragged herself to the kitchen. She fell into her chair and put her head down. Jordan's mother walked in and asked how her first week of fifth grade had been.

"Just fabulous. An unbelievable week," Jordan sighed.

"It doesn't sound like it. How is your teacher? Have you made any new friends yet?"

"The kids in the class are super nice, but my teacher is mean! You should see the overwhelming amount of homework she assigned!"

Jordan went and got the planner from her backpack and opened it on the kitchen table so they could look at it together. Jordan had assignments in each subject, but none of them were due until the following Friday. As a matter of fact, most of her subjects only had one assignment, and none of them were very tedious.

"Jordan, honey, take a look at this. Your spelling is a BINGO card, but you only have to complete four of the choices. In social studies, you have three pages to read and one question to answer for each page. In science, you have to complete a graphic organizer. There's a reading log to fill out, but you already read every night anyway! And, in math you have 50 problems, but that isn't even 10 each day. That may seem like a lot, but if we come up with a plan, I'm sure it won't take very long. Let's make a list and you can decide what to tackle each day. What do you think?"

"Thanks, Mom! When you put it that way, it really doesn't seem like much."

Name _____

Answer the questions.

1. What lesson can you learn from "The Crow and the Pitcher"?

_____

_____

2. Use two words to describe Crow. Support each word with text evidence.

_____

_____

3. How does Jordan change from the beginning of "Do I Have To?" to the end?

_____

_____

4. What causes Jordan to change?

_____

_____

5. Imagine that Crow was the main character in "Do I Have To?" How do you think the story would be different?

_____

_____

6. What do you think Jordan will do the next time she is discouraged and facing a problem? Why do you think this?

_____

_____

_____

_____

7. Using information from both passages, complete the following chart.

	Problem	**Solution**	**Lesson/Moral**
The Crow and the Pitcher			
Do I Have To?			

8. Using the table above, write a summary of each story. Be sure to highlight the similarities between the passages.

_____

_____

_____

_____

_____

_____

_____

_____

The Ant and the Grasshopper
by Aesop (adapted)

In a field one summer's day, Grasshopper was hopping about, chirping and singing to his heart's content. Ant passed by, carrying along with great **toil** an ear of corn he was taking to the nest.

"Why not come and chat with me," said Grasshopper, "instead of toiling and working in that way?"

"I am helping lay up food for the winter," said Ant, "and I recommend that you do the same."

"Why bother about winter?" said Grasshopper. "We have got plenty of food at present." But, Ant went on his way and continued his toil.

When the winter came, Grasshopper had no food and found himself dying of hunger. Every day, he saw the ants distributing corn and grain from the stores they had collected in the summer.

Then, Grasshopper knew: It is best to prepare for the days of necessity.

All Play and No Work

"And don't forget your book reports are due on Monday!" Mrs. Rivera called out to the class as they noisily exited her classroom.

Terrance barely heard Mrs. Rivera as he ran out of the classroom Friday afternoon. He couldn't wait for the weekend! Hours of video games, sports, TV, and hanging out with friends awaited him. Andrew would be over at 5 pm and, after a quick neighborhood basketball game, the boys were going to order pizza and play the newest video game until the wee hours of the morning. They both intended to make it to the next level before heading to bed. Terrance was looking forward to the evening!

By the time they got up Saturday, it was time for lunch. Andrew went home and Terrance called Nassim. He said he couldn't come over since he was reading the final three chapters of the book he had chosen for his report. Terrance hung up and went outside to find someone else. A few of the older boys were getting a game of soccer going and Terrance joined in until dinner. After eating, the family played a board game and watched a movie.

Sunday rolled around and Terrance's family went to church and out to lunch with friends. After such a busy weekend, he decided to take a quick nap before tackling the next level of his new video game. After showering and eating dinner, his mom helped him get things ready for school the next day.

A book fell out of his backpack as he was loading it. "Oh no," thought Terrance, "now what am I going to do? I totally forgot about the book report!"

Name _____

Answer the questions.

1. What is the author's purpose for writing "The Ant and the Grasshopper"?

_____

_____

2. What does the word **toil** mean as used in "The Ant and the Grasshopper"?

    A. play   **B.** work   **C.** walk   **D.** help

3. What is the main idea of "All Play and No Work"?

_____

4. What is the problem in "All Play and No Work"?

_____

5. Which sentence from the story best sums up the problem?

    A. Terrance barely heard Mrs. Rivera as he ran out of the classroom Friday afternoon.

    B. Andrew would be over at 5 pm and, after a quick neighborhood basketball game, the boys were going to order pizza and play the newest video game until the wee hours of the morning.

    C. He said he couldn't come over since he was reading the final three chapters of the book he had chosen for his report.

    D. I totally forgot about the book report!

6. Circle the five most important words in "The Ant and the Grasshopper." Why did you choose those words?

_____

_____

_____

_____

Name _____

7. Circle the five most important words in "All Play and No Work." Why did you choose those words?

_____

_____

8. Compare and contrast both stories. Use the graphic organizer to record your thinking.

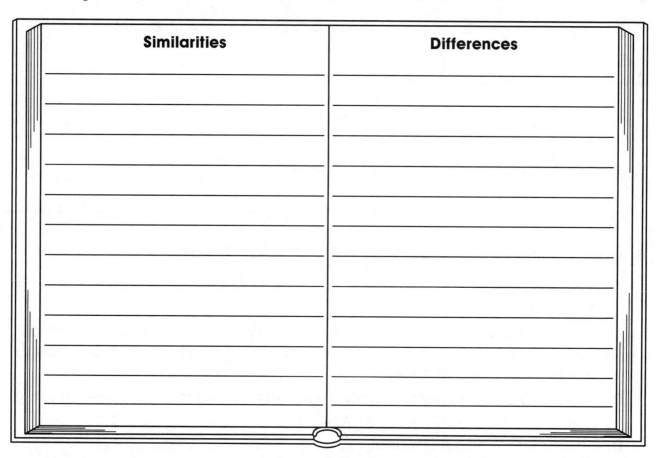

Similarities	Differences

9. Pretend you are the grasshopper. Write a letter to Terrance that you will deliver to him on Saturday morning.

_____

_____

_____

_____

_____

76

Day Seven

Arianna was so excited! She was old enough to help light one of the Kwanzaa candles. Her brothers and sisters had been helping for as long as she could remember. Tonight it was her turn! Every member of her family was around the table. The candles were in the stand on the *mkeka*, or place mat. The six from earlier in the week were already burning brightly in the dim room. Granny reminded us that this is important because it is part of our culture.

Arianna remembered the first night. Daddy lit the unity candle and spoke about everyone being together. Rashad got to light the next two candles, since he was the oldest. He even talked about having self-determination his first night. He talked about working together on his second night.

Kenyon lit the next two. Granny helped him talk about opening stores in our community on his first night. He said his favorite was the ice cream shop up the street! On his second night, Momma helped with the candle. They talked about having a purpose, although Arianna couldn't remember what that meant.

Ebony, just one year older than Arianna, lit one on the sixth night. Rashad helped her. He talked about being creative and making things beautiful.

Daddy picked up Arianna and held her up to the table. Momma helped her light her candle. She said it was about faith—that meant to believe with all our hearts. Because it was the final night, Rashad began playing a drum. Granny sang an old song from when she was a little girl. Arianna's insides were burning as brightly as the candles!

Hanukkah!

Joshua and Rebecca listened as Papa told them all about the candles in front of them. He explained that they would celebrate and remember for the next eight nights. Over 2,000 years ago, the Jewish people living in Judea were told they could not practice their religion. They were told to begin worshipping other gods, and their temple was taken over.

After many years, the Jewish people won back control of their temple and they went in to light the menorah (candle holder). They were to light all seven candles. The candles stood for knowledge and creation and were to burn brightly. There was a big problem, though. There was only enough oil for one night. The people lit the candles and a miracle happened. The candles burned for eight nights! This was long enough to find more oil.

Papa said that, in memory of this time, the eight candles on the holder would be lit. Mama would be making potato pancakes. After dinner, there would be a game with the wooden dreidel. Then, before bed, the first night's gifts would be given.

Rebecca jumped up and down in excitement. Joshua asked his papa if he could help light the candles. Papa agreed, but told him that they only light one candle on the first night. Tomorrow, they would light another candle and Rebecca would help. Joshua was ready for Hanukkah to begin!

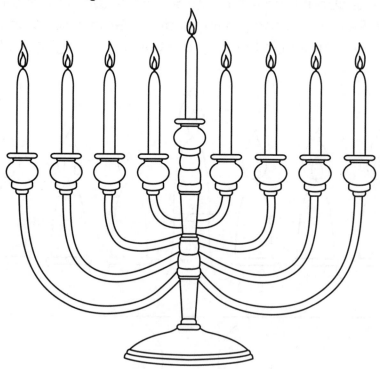

Name _____

Answer the questions.

1. What is the main idea of "Day Seven"?

_____

_____

2. What is the importance of the candles in "Day Seven"?

_____

_____

3. How was Arianna feeling at the end of "Day Seven"? How do you know?

_____

_____

_____

4. What is the main idea of "Hanukkah!"?

_____

_____

5. What is the importance of the candles in "Hanukkah!"?

_____

_____

6. What do you think will happen on day three of Hanukkah? Explain your thinking.

_____

_____

_____

_____

_____

Name _____

7. Think about Kwanzaa and Hanukkah. How are they similar? How are they different? Complete the organizer below.

Kwanzaa   **Hanukkah**

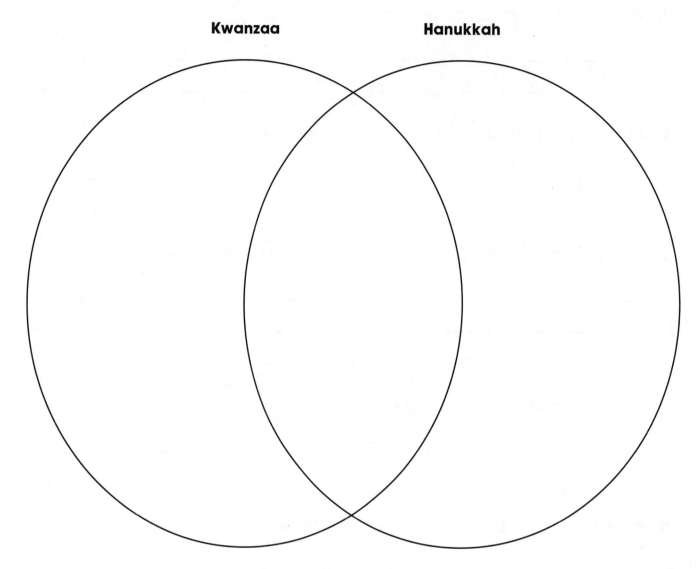

8. Use the information from the organizer to summarize both holidays.

_____

_____

_____

_____

_____

_____

Up and At It in Japan

Yuri's alarm wakes him at 6:00 am. He gets out of bed and wakes up his little brother. He and his mom begin cooking breakfast: miso, fish, rice, and vegetables. By 7:30 am, he leaves home to meet his friends. They begin their 25-minute walk to school in a single-file line. Once at school, he removes his shoes at the door and steps into his "indoor shoes."

At 8:30 am, the morning meeting has begun. The principal leads this and the teachers take attendance. Yuri's first class, mathematics, begins at 8:50 am. He works on multiplication problems. Science begins at 9:50 am. He is studying the atmosphere and weather. At 10:50 am, he and his classmates change clothing for gym. They do group stretching and then participate in volleyball games. After changing back into their clothes, the class heads to writing class. Each child is working on copying Chinese symbols. Yuri uses a special ink and paper for this.

When the clock says 12:50 pm, it means lunchtime. It is Yuri's turn to serve. He and three classmates bring the food to the classroom and pass it out. After lunch, everyone helps to clean the classroom. Once that is finished, they all join the other students to clean the school. When the clock says 1:50 pm, it's time for Japanese class, where he learns about the culture and history of his country.

Once this is finished, Yuri's brother goes home. Yuri stays for his soccer club, which meets three times per week. Then, he will head home to complete homework and, if there's time, play a video game. He will help his father prepare dinner, and then Yuri will eat, bathe, and go to bed.

School Days

Miguel lives in Florida. His alarm goes off at 6:45 am. He gets up, takes a shower, and heads downstairs. By 7:45 am, he is at the table eating a bowl of cereal. His mom packs his lunch and hands him his backpack. He walks down to the corner to catch the bus. Miguel arrives at school at 8:30 am and unpacks at his desk. At 8:45 am, the tardy bell rings, and the class stands up for the Pledge of Allegiance. The principal gives the day's announcements, and the teacher takes attendance.

Math begins at 8:50 am. Miguel is working on word problems and fractions. He then pulls out his reading book. His teacher is helping the class learn more about drawing conclusions today. After this, the class works on word study with new vocabulary and finishes writing their opinion essays.

At noon, the class walks to the cafeteria for lunch. Miguel doesn't like any of the choices today, so he has brought his own lunch. After eating, they head outside for recess. The boys gather for a game of soccer. The boys are having fun, so recess is over before they know it. At 1:00 pm, they head in and work on social studies. At 1:45 pm, they go to music class. Once they return to the classroom, they finish the day with science. The dismissal bell rings at 3:30 pm.

Miguel is anxious to get home so that he can play video games and watch TV until his parents get home. He completes his homework while his mom makes dinner. After eating, he watches a movie with his parents and heads to bed.

Name _____

Answer the questions.

1. What is the text structure of "Up and At It in Japan"?

   A. cause/effect   **B.** description

   C. chronology   **D.** problem/solution

2. How old do you think Yuri is? Support your answer with evidence from the passage.

   _____

   _____

   _____

3. What can you conclude about school in Japan? Use text evidence to support your answer.

   _____

   _____

   _____

4. Which text feature could the author of "School Days" have included to make the information easier to understand? Explain your thinking.

   _____

   _____

   _____

5. Would you rather attend school in Japan or Florida? Use text evidence to support your opinion.

   _____

   _____

   _____

   _____

Name _____

6. Think about the information in both passages. Create a schedule for both boys.

Yuri		Miguel	
Time	Activity	Time	Activity

7. Using the information in the schedules you created, write two paragraphs comparing and contrasting Yuri and Miguel's days.

_____

_____

_____

_____

_____

_____

_____

_____

The Fox and the Geese
Based on the Brothers Grimm Tale

Characters: Fox   Goose 1   Goose 2   Goose 3   Narrator

Narrator: One spring day in a meadow . . .

Fox: *(rubbing his paws together and smiling)* I see I have come at just the right time! You are all here looking so beautiful together. I will eat you all up, one after the other!

All Geese: *(flutters wings and honk in terror)*

Goose 2: *(continues to flutter wings)* Oh, oh, oh, Mr. Fox! I have children at home!

Goose 3: *(continues to flutter wings)* I beg you, kind sir, please leave us be!

Fox: There is no **mercy** to be had! I am quite hungry and you all must die!

Goose 1: If that is our fate, please allow us one small favor.

Goose 2: All we ask is that we may pray before we die.

Goose 3: We will then place ourselves in a row and you may pick out the fattest to begin your feast.

Fox: Yes, that is a reasonable request. Pray away and I will wait until you are finished.

Goose 1: *(quietly, with wings together, head bowed, and eyes closed)* Honk, honk, honk, honk *(continue honking quietly until play has ended)*.

Goose 2: *(quietly joins in after six or seven honks from Goose 1, with wings together, head bowed, and eyes closed)* Honk, honk, honk, honk *(continue honking quietly until play has ended)*.

Goose 3: *(quietly joins in after six or seven honks from Goose 2, with wings together, head bowed, and eyes closed)* Honk, honk, honk, honk *(continue honking quietly until play has ended)*.

Fox: *(begins tapping foot after Goose 1 honks a few times; sit down after Goose 2 honks a few times; lay down after Goose 3 honks a few times)*.

Narrator: *(begins speaking loudly after Fox has lain down)* And as you sit here listening to this tale, the geese are honking still to this day!

The Fox and the Crow
by Aesop (adapted)

Characters: Fox   Crow   Narrator

(a "piece of cheese" should be placed on the stage in plain sight)

Narrator: One beautiful spring day . . .

Crow: Oh, how I love to fly on a day such as this! Look at that piece of cheese just lying there for the taking! And, after so much flying, I am quite **famished**. I will grab that up for myself. *(flaps wings and "flies" to cheese; picks it up in "beak"; flaps wings and "flies" to an elevated seat)*

Fox: *(across the stage, speaking quietly)* That cheese should be mine, as I am a fox! *(crawls across stage to the seat and smiles while looking up at Crow; speaks in a very friendly voice)* Good day, Miss Crow! How fine you are looking today. Your feathers are so glossy; your eyes are so bright. I am sure your voice must surpass that of any other bird, as your beauty is far more than any other. Please let me hear just one song from you so that I may greet you as the Queen of Birds.

Crow: *(lifts head and opens mouth to sing)* La-la-la-la-la-la-la-la-la!

Fox: *(bends down and quickly picks up the piece of cheese)* That will do. This was all I wanted. *(turn around and slowly crawl off stage)*

Narrator: *(looks to Crow)* A piece of advice for the future: Never trust one who flatters you!

Name _____

Answer the questions.

1. What genre is "The Fox and the Geese"? Support your answer with evidence.

_____

_____

2. What does the word **mercy** mean as used in "The Fox and the Geese"?

   A. dinner   **B.** kindness   **C.** anger   **D.** trick

3. Look back at the ending of "The Fox and the Geese." What is the author's purpose for ending the play this way? Support your answer.

_____

_____

_____

4. What is the author's purpose for writing "The Fox and the Crow"? Support your answer.

_____

_____

5. What does the word **famished** mean as used in "The Fox and the Crow"?

   A. hungry   **B.** tired   **C.** ready   **D.** finished

6. The narrator in "The Fox and the Crow" states, *"Never trust one who flatters you!"* What is meant by this? Explain how you know.

_____

_____

_____

_____

_____

Name _____

7. Throughout history, authors have used foxes in stories in many ways. Think about the ways that a fox character is used in these plays and complete the organizer below.

	The Fox and the Crow	**The Fox and the Geese**
Character Trait		
Evidence		

8. Use the chart above to write a conversation between the fox in "The Fox and the Geese" and the one in "The Fox and the Crow." Pretend that the conversation is happening the day after each event took place.

_____

_____

_____

_____

_____

_____

_____

_____

_____

Broken

Liv grabbed her bag and came running down the stairs. As she ran around the corner, she accidentally knocked her mom's vase off the table. It tumbled to the floor. Liv turned around and gasped: the vase laid there in pieces. Her mother would be so furious! Her mother had gotten it as a gift from her best friend after having talked of wanting it for months.

As Liv walked over to clean it up, she realized that no one else was at home. She bent over and began picking up the pieces. Maybe she could somehow put it back together and her mother would never find out. She went into the kitchen and grabbed the glue from the desk. Then, she made an emergency call to her friend Wendy to ask her to come over and help.

Liv and Wendy worked for over an hour making sure every piece was right where it belonged. It was like putting a puzzle together, making sure each piece fit exactly where it belonged. When they were finished, the vase didn't look quite the same but you had to pick it up to really see what was wrong. Liv placed it back on the front table and hoped for the best.

She was supposed to babysit that night for her neighbors. The Patels and the Contis had asked her to watch their children all day on Saturday. If she saved every penny she made and took a little from her bank account, she could sneak to the store and buy a new one. She'd switch vases and no one would be the wiser. She just hoped the store still carried the same vase.

Lost

Owen was on the bus heading home when he reached into his backpack to grab his house key. Mom and Dad had just given it to him last week at the beginning of fifth grade because they finally trusted him to come home all by himself! Although it had been a little terrifying at first, Owen loved that little bit of time alone, with no one telling him what to do! He also was proud that his parents were giving him more responsibility and not treating him like a baby anymore. His friends from school, Zach and Michaela, had been staying home alone for two years already.

Owen felt around, then felt panicky. The key was not in its usual spot. Owen **frantically** opened the other pockets and looked through all of them but no matter where he looked, the key wasn't there. What had happened to it and how would he get in? He knew that when Mom and Dad found out, they would be irritated and probably put him back in the after-school program.

Then, Owen remembered one day last year when he and Dad had gone to the park. Mom wasn't home when they returned, and Dad had to get the spare key from under the plant on the back patio. Owen looked under the plant. Sure enough, the key was still there. He unlocked the door and then put the key back. Maybe Owen could do that every day and they'd never find out!

Owen was happy with his solution to the problem today. But, the more he thought about it, the more sure he became that he'd tell them about the missing key. If he didn't and they found out, he'd be in even more trouble.

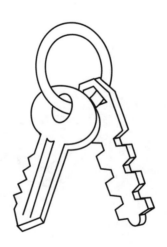

Name _____

Answer the questions.

I. Summarize "Broken" in your own words.

_____

_____

_____

2. Think of two words you would use to describe Liv. Use evidence from the passage to support your answer.

_____

_____

_____

3. The author of "Broken" ends by stating that "no one would be the wiser." What is meant by this?

_____

_____

4. What is the theme of "Lost"? Which details from the story support the theme?

_____

_____

_____

5. Think of two words you would use to describe Owen. Use evidence from the story to support your answer.

_____

_____

_____

6. What does the word **frantically** mean as used in "Lost"?

A. calmly   **B.** desperately   **C.** easily   **D.** loudly

Name _____

7. Think about both stories and complete the organizer below.

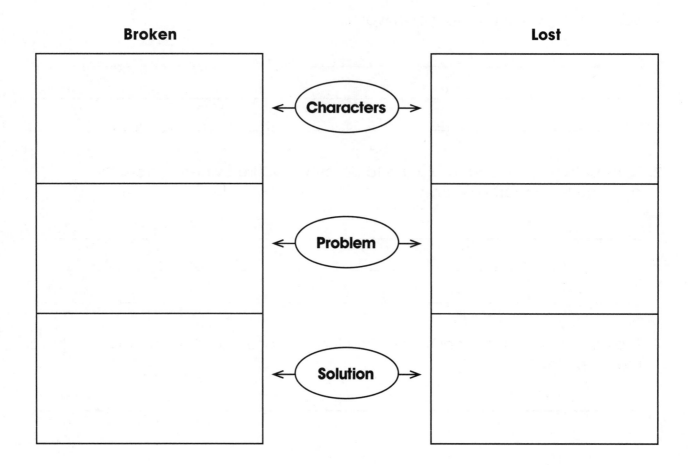

Broken   **Lost**

Characters

Problem

Solution

8. Think about the graphic organizer above and what you have learned about Liv and Owen. Write a paragraph telling what you think about their decisions. Support your opinions with evidence from the passages.

_____

_____

_____

_____

_____

_____

_____

_____

Answer Key

Pages 7–8
1. Poem; Answers will vary but should include elements of poetry. 2. List; Answers will vary but should include the numbered steps. 3. Answers will vary but should include text evidence. 4. Fall; Answers will vary but may include yellow wood and leaves on ground. 5. Making decisions is difficult but there are things that you can do to make it easier. 6. C; 7. Answers will vary but should include at least two steps and text evidence from the poem. 8. Answers will vary but should incorporate both passages and show understanding of the decision-making process.

Pages 11–12
1. The wind believes that he controls the moon. 2. Answers will vary but should include evidence from the poem. 3. A; 4. Answers will vary. 5. lit; "from the sun"; 6. Answers will vary but should include evidence from poem. 7. new = 2, 6; first quarter=3, 7, 8; full = 9; third quarter = 5; 8. Answers will vary.

Pages 15–16
1. C; 2. Teasing is done in fun with friends or family, and bullying is meant to be mean and the person won't stop. 3. B; 4. Answers will vary but may include that she was mad and tried to get back at the bully. 5. Answers will vary. 6. Answers will vary but should include evidence from both passages. 7. Answers will vary.

Pages 19–20
1. Check students' work. 2. Answers will vary. 3. It was not being used anymore. 4. Answers will vary but should include that Robert did not mean to break the bell. 5. idiom; Children should not speak unless spoken to. 6. Answers will vary. 7. nonfiction, It should contain facts about the Liberty Bell. fiction, It should show the story is not true. 8. Answers will vary.

Pages 23–24
1. Children in New York City without parents were placed on trains that took them west in the hopes that they would be taken in by farmers throughout America. 2. C; 3. Answers will vary. 4. Answers will vary but may include that it tells the story of a 12-year-old boy on an orphan train who wants to be taken in to a real home. 5. Answers will vary but may include that the boy wants someone to take him in and thinks that being nice and saying please may help. 6. Answers will vary. 7. Answers will vary but may include the author of "Orphan Trains" believes they were a good thing and the narrator of "Please?" isn't sure that the orphan trains are good. Students should include evidence from the text. 8. Answers will vary.

Pages 27–28
1. thine alabaster cities gleam; for amber waves of grain, above the fruited plain; for purple mountain majesties;

2. Answers will vary but may include the Revolutionary War. 3. stampeding buffalo like drums in my ears (the buffalo were very loud); lakes as still and clear as a sheet of glass (very still and clear); mountains so tall it'd take weeks to cross them (very tall mountains); 4. Answers will vary but may include reference to their ages or the responsibility of being a mother or father. 5. Answers will vary but should include fields, meadows, lakes, cities, and mountains and corresponding emotions. 6. Answers will vary.

Pages 31–32
1. Answers will vary but may include where he grew up or the fact that so many of his siblings died. 2. the boys reform school; 3. C; 4. Answers will vary but may include not giving up. 5. Ruby was in an accident that caused her to be in a wheelchair but her brother helped her to learn to play basketball again. 6. Answers will vary. 7. A; 8. Answers will vary. 9. Answers will vary but should include details about Babe Ruth turning his life around and Ruby working hard and not giving up.

Pages 35–36
1. C; 2. D; 3. B; 4. A; 5. A; 6. Only a small amount is used in those products; 7. The eucalyptus tree is very useful in daily life, both for animals and people. 8. Answers will vary. 9. Answers will vary.

Answer Key

Pages 39–40

1. Cell phones cause many accidents every year. 2. 1.6 million accidents are caused by cell phone use and 330,000 people are injured in the accidents. 3. Many students ride a school bus and it is a normal part of the day. 4. 25 million students ride the bus and they don't even pay attention. 5. The cell phone is what caused the car accident the family was in. 6. to show that it is a normal thing and that is why students typically don't pay attention on the bus; 7. Answers will vary. 8. Answers will vary but might include words like brave, caring, and determined.

Pages 43–44

1. A; 2. Exercise is key to good health. 3. Answers will vary. 4. C; 5. The author talks about how exercise helps with your mood and your brain. 6. to remind kids that exercise is an important part of daily life and can help improve health; 7. Answers will vary but should include evidence from the passage. 8. Answers will vary but should include the fact that exercise is good for you.

Pages 47–48

1. D; 2. The first settlement to Roanoke disappeared and no one knows what happened to them. 3. Answers will vary but may include that Roanoke was truly the first American settlement, that when White returned the settlement was deserted, or that the settlement disappeared and

no one ever heard from them again. 4. to tell the story about two unusual children who appeared in a village and were green; 5. Both stories are about events that cannot be explained. 6. One is about a settlement of people who disappeared and one is about a brother and sister who suddenly appeared out of nowhere. 7. B; 8. Answers will vary. 9. Answers will vary.

Pages 51–52

1. lighting – to see where the shore is; mirrors – the light is brighter; rotating lights – helps to know the lighthouse; daymark – helps to see the lighthouse during the day; 2. B; 3. Answers will vary but may include the way the lights rotate and shine off and on. 4. Answers will vary. 5. A; 6. The water in the sea is always moving, when it is stormy it can be very loud. 7. "Light the Night" = main, evidence should reference all the improvements to lighthouses; "Keep the Light Burning, Abbie" = supporting, evidence should reference the fact that the main character is Abbie and that the story is all about her bravery during the storm. 8. Answers will vary.

Pages 55–56

1. to explain how and why Benjamin Franklin invented lightning rods; 2. Answers will vary but may include that he was constantly thinking, that he studied electricity and lightning, that he worked to

prove his theory, or that he invented the lightning rod. 3. Answers will vary but may include that it has prevented many buildings from catching fire during storms. 4. to explain facts about lightning and to give suggestions for what to do during storms; 5. A; 6. Answers will vary. 7. "What Was That?"– Ben Franklin proved that lightning was electricity and then invented a lightning rod to help prevent buildings from catching fire during storms. Supporting details will vary. "A Powerful Force" – Lightning is very powerful and causes many fires and injuries every year so people should be careful when caught outside during a storm. Supporting details will vary. 8. Answers will vary.

Pages 59–60

1. Answers will vary but may include because many American Indians died and the journey was very difficult so it was a sad time. 2. Answers will vary but may include that the author believes it was a bad thing to do to the American Indians. The author talks about how many died, the sickness, the fact that they left with very little, and ends by stating that it is a sad time in American history. 3. Answers will vary but may include the fact that the Supreme Court ruled in their favor or that they were there first and the land was theirs. 4. The Underground Railroad is an important part of history that helped to free thousands of slaves during

Answer Key

the 1800s. 5. Answers will vary. 6. Answers will vary but may include that it would be easier to sneak and not be seen at night. Answers will vary but may include that it would be difficult to see and would be scary. 7. "Trail of Tears" – travel was forced and the Indians were being led away from freedom, they were forced to go, the journey was difficult, people died along the way, they lost their homes; "The Underground Railroad" – travel was by choice and the slaves were being led toward freedom, people helped them along the way, the journey was their choice; 8. Answers will vary.

Pages 63–64
1. D; 2. B; 3. Answers will vary. 4. A; 5. Adam had his heart broken. This means that someone caused him to feel very sad because they broke up with him. 6. Answers will vary but similarities should include working hard at an early age, dropping out of college, and becoming successful. 7. Answers will vary but should include working hard and not giving up.

Pages 67–68
1. C; 2. B; 3. D; 4. C; 5. B; 6. Answers will vary but may include that they both worked very hard and were very tired. 7. Answers will vary but may include that Sara worked in and around the house and barn and the narrator of the poem worked at picking apples all day. 8. Answers

will vary but may include hard-working, responsible, or helpful. 9. Answers will vary.

Pages 71–72
1. Answers will vary but may include the fact that you should never give up or that there's always a solution if you think about it. 2. Answers will vary but may include smart, creative, hard-working, or determined. 3. At the beginning she is frustrated but at the end she is encouraged. 4. Her mother helps her to come up with a plan. 5. Answers will vary but may include that Crow would not have complained. Crow would have thought and come up with a solution. 6. Answers will vary but may include talking to her mother or thinking about a solution. 7. "The Crow and the Pitcher"– The problem is that Crow is half-dead with thirst. The solution is to put one pebble at a time into the pitcher until the water is high enough to drink. "Do I Have To?" – The problem is that Jordan has a lot of homework and is overwhelmed. The solution is to break the homework into a little bit each day. The lessons or morals will vary but should be linked logically to the stories. 8. Answers will vary but should include working a little at a time to solve a problem.

Pages 75–76
1. to show that you need to do the work necessary in order to prevent trouble in the future; 2. B; 3. Terrance played all

weekend long, even though he had a report due. He forgot about the report until Sunday night, when it was too late to finish it. 4. Terrance had a book report he didn't complete. 5. D; 6. Answers will vary. 7. Answers will vary. 8. Answers will vary but should include the fact that one character works and has what is needed while another character plays and is not prepared. 9. Answers will vary.

Pages 79–80
1. Kwanzaa is a special holiday that is celebrated for seven days. Each day has a candle with a special meaning to it. 2. They are about unity, self-determination, working together, community stores, having a purpose, being creative, and faith. 3. Answers will vary but may include that she was very excited. Her insides were burning as brightly as the candles. 4. Hanukkah is a special holiday that lasts eight days. It is celebrated to help remember the miracle of the oil lasting for eight days. 5. The candles help to remind people that the oil that should have lasted only one day lasted for eight days. 6. The family will light three candles. On day one, they lit one candle. On day two, they lit two candles. 7. Answers will vary but the similarities should include candles being lit each day, one at a time, and the fact that they are celebrations families participate in together. The differences should include

Answer Key

what the candles represent and the number of nights each celebration lasts. 8. Answers will vary.

Pages 83–84

1. C; 2. Answers will vary but should refer to a school age. 3. Answers will vary. 4. Answers will vary but may include a timeline, schedule, or chart. 5. Answers will vary. 6. Answers will vary but should include all the times and activities listed. 7. Answers will vary but should include similar classes, video games, breakfast, lunch, dinner, and bed. Differences should include the types of classes, lunch and breakfast food, the help given at home, and length of school day.

Pages 87–88

1. It is a play. It includes characters and stage directions. 2. B; 3. to help the audience understand that the geese were never eaten; 4. to teach a lesson—that you should be careful when someone is being too nice; 5. A; 6. Answers will vary but should include that if someone is being too nice, they may want something from you. 7. "The Fox and the Geese"—foolish, he allowed the geese to keep honking and avoid being eaten; "The Fox and the Crow" – smart, he tricked the crow into dropping the cheese so he could eat it; 8. Answers will vary.

Pages 91–92

1. Answers will vary but should include that Liv broke her mother's vase and had her friend help her put it back together. She decided to secretly replace it and never tell her mom. 2. Answers will vary but may include sneaky, untrustworthy, or clever. 3. No one would ever know what she'd done. 4. Answers will vary but may include that when you have a problem or have done something wrong, it is best to be honest about it. 5. Answers will vary but may include honest, trustworthy, or smart. 6. B; 7. "Broken" – Liv and Wendy, mom's vase got broken, glue it back together and replace it before anyone finds out; "Lost" – Owen, he lost his key, use the spare key for today and be honest with his parents; 8. Answers will vary.